Aphrodite's Magic

Celebrate and Heal Your Sexuality

First published by O Books, 2010
O Books is an imprint of John Hunt Publishing Ltd., The Bothy, Deershot Lodge, Park Lane, Ropley,
Hants, SO24 0BE, UK
office1@o-books.net
www.o-books.net

Distribution in:	South Africa
	Stephan Phillips (pty) Ltd
UK and Europe	Email: orders@stephanphillips.com
Orca Book Services	Tel: 27 21 4489839 Telefax: 27 21 4479879
orders@orcabookservices.co.uk	
Tel: 01202 665432 Fax: 01202 666219	Text copyright Jane Meredith 2009
Int. code (44)	
	Design: Stuart Davies
USA and Canada	
NBN	ISBN: 978 1 84694 286 0
custserv@nbnbooks.com	
Tel: 1 800 462 6420 Fax: 1 800 338 4550	All rights reserved. Except for brief quotations
	in critical articles or reviews, no part of this
Australia and New Zealand	book may be reproduced in any manner without
Brumby Books	prior written permission from the publishers.
sales@brumbybooks.com.au	
Tel: 61 3 9761 5535 Fax: 61 3 9761 7095	The rights of Jane Meredith as author have
	been asserted in accordance with the
Far East (offices in Singapore, Thailand,	Copyright, Designs and Patents Act 1988.
Hong Kong, Taiwan)	
Pansing Distribution Pte Ltd	
kemal@pansing.com	A CIP catalogue record for this book is available
Tel: 65 6319 9939 Fax: 65 6462 5761	from the British Library.

Printed by Digital Book Print

O Books operates a distinctive and ethical publishing philosophy in
all areas of its business, from its global network of authors to
production and worldwide distribution.

Aphrodite's Magic

Celebrate and Heal Your Sexuality

Jane Meredith

BOOKS

Winchester, UK
Washington, USA

CONTENTS

Dedication   vii
Acknowledgements   viii

Invitation to the Magic   1

Before You Begin: Practical Guidelines   6

First Strand: The Goddess   20
Second Strand: Eye of Beauty   43
Third Strand: Voice of Truth   61
Fourth Strand: In the Heart   78
Fifth Strand: Dancing the Body   96
Sixth Stand: Red Womb   114
Seventh Strand: Inner Mysteries   133

Weaving Aphrodite's Magic   155

Afterword: Living with Aphrodite's Magic   165

About the Author   170

Aphrodite's Magic goes far above and beyond being a regular sex manual. It's a recipe book showing us how to become women of more wisdom and power. Not recommended for the cynical and closed-minded.
Annie Sprinkle, Ph.D., Sexologist, Artist

Full of tenderness, tears, laughter, creativity and dance – all wrapped up in the velvet candlelit gorgeousness of a sensual magical spell –
Emma Restall Orr, Druid, author of *Kissing the Hag*

I applaud Jane Meredith's approach to dealing with what is still a taboo subject for Western society... Aphrodite's Magic is a pathway for a woman to being one step closer to who she is in her body and sexuality.
Elise Julien, Ph.D., Clinical and Counseling Psychologist

An exceptional resource for women on a quest for healing, balance and discovering the source of pure love lying within.
Diana Richardson, Acclaimed Tantra teacher,
author of *The Heart of Tantric Sex*

Aphrodite's Magic is a great book about sexuality, self expression and freedom for women. It's a magical spellbinding book that can change women's lives.
Kathy Jones, Glastonbury Goddess Conference Organizer,
author of *Priestess of Avalon, Priestess of the Goddess*

*This book is dedicated to the Goddess Aphrodite
and the healing and celebration of women's sexuality
all over the earth*

With thanks to:

Annabell, Artemesia, Berin, Catriona, Deb, Diane, Gini,
Golden, Helen, Jenny, Kate, Miriam, Shelley and Tanna
who completed Aphrodite's Magic, made girdles,
filled in questionnaires and continue to dance the dances
of their own sexuality and of the Goddess.

ACKNOWLEDGEMENTS

Page 24: Quote from Donald Russell's translation of Plutarch's *Advice to the Bride and Groom*. Published in *Plutarch's Advice to the Bride and Groom and A Consolation to his Wife: English Translations, commentary, Interpretive Essays, and Bibliography*, edited: Sarah B. Pomeroy. Published: Oxford University Press US, 1999.

Page 133: Quote from Eve Einsler's *The Vagina Monologues*. Villard, 2007

Jane Meredith's website is: www.janemeredith.com
She can be contacted at: jane@janemeredith.com

INVITATION TO THE MAGIC

Aphrodite's Magic is a magical spell.

Aphrodite, Goddess of love and sexuality was known in ancient times for her beauty, sensuality and sexual freedom. She owned a magical girdle – a belt worn low about the hips – which was forged from precious metals and gave powers of irresistible sexual attraction to whoever wore it.

We have lost our understanding of the essential power and beauty of women's sexuality. Most women do not believe they are beautiful. Many women have a sexual history of pain, abuse, and broken hearts and we have not been taught to heal our personal suffering. We do not know how to celebrate our sexuality. Being a woman carries a whole culture's restrictions of the feminine and very few women revel in their body as a manifestation of the Goddess. We live in a place without Temples.

This book will take you into the Temple. *Aphrodite's Magic* will support you to discover your inherent beauty and your enormous potential to change and heal. You will learn to embody the celebration of your sexuality; through dance, journalling and ritual. If you wish, you can make your own Aphrodite's Girdle.

Aphrodite's Magic came to life as I was sitting on a bench in Glastonbury High Street. I was searching for a way women could relate to their sexuality; not through their relationships with their lovers, partners or children – or lack of them – but within themselves. The story of Aphrodite's magical girdle tempted me. I could sense the movement of it, swirling about her hips. I saw a Temple building itself around her dance. I heard faint music, whispered chants. I had spent many years dedicated to the Dark Goddess but, in my own life, sexuality had been a strong theme.

The bright colors and movement of Aphrodite beckoned me.

I ran my first Aphrodite workshop at the Glastonbury Goddess Conference in 2001 with twenty women. We made Aphrodite Girdles by weaving together seven cords, each one linked to a process of healing and celebrating our sexuality. Women wore their girdles to the Conference Ball, they wore them to rituals, they wore them in the High Street and they wore them home.

I've run the workshop many times since then; so I don't know how many girdles exist in the world. But I know there aren't enough. Aphrodite's own girdle represented her intrinsic qualities of self-defined sexuality, radiant beauty and sensual freedom. The girdles made in *Aphrodite's Magic* symbolize each woman's reclaiming of those essential qualities. One by one, we are weaving Aphrodite's Magic.

When I sat down to write this book I was supported by the comments of fourteen women who had completed the workshop and filled in an extensive questionnaire. Their comments appear throughout *Aphrodite's Magic*. They write about their girdles, the processes they went though and the changes they have undergone as a result of this work. Their voices are individual, moving, contentious, personal. They are heterosexual and lesbian and celibate. They are grandmothers, mothers and women who have never borne a child. They range in age from their twenties to their sixties. They live in Australia, the United Kingdom and Europe and five of them have a language other than English as their first language.

Your own journey into *Aphrodite's Magic* begins when you invoke a Temple and continues through seven aspects of your sexuality. These are linked to the chakras, seven energy centers of the body that are acknowledged in many cultures and healing traditions. *Aphrodite's Magic* begins with the crown chakra, representing your connection to the divine and descends through the body to finish with the root chakra, grounding you into your body, the earth and this physical existence.

In the spell of *Aphrodite's Magic* you gather one cord for your own girdle at each of the seven levels. Each cord is infused with your intention, ritual and personal magic and when you weave them together into a girdle, your magical spell is complete. The girdle can be worn for dance or ritual and is also a beautiful object to decorate your Altar or bedroom.

If you don't feel ready to take on the whole *Aphrodite's Magic* spell just yet, you may choose to enjoy some of the rituals and processes or simply to read the book. You can use the different chapters to learn about aspects of your sexuality, your relationship to your body and your intrinsic magic. At any stage you can begin the spell that will result in your own magical girdle.

In Aphrodite's Temple it doesn't matter what age you are, what your sexual orientation is or what your life experience has been. But it does matter that you choose to embrace your feminine self and undertake the journey of discovering your sexuality. It matters that you decide these things are worthy of your time and attention. Your commitment to celebrating and healing aspects of yourself and your sexuality as they arise is the essence of this spell.

If you have particular issues around sexuality – they might include a history of sexual abuse or incest; fear of intimacy; a poor body image; infertility; aging; an unconventional sexual orientation or lifestyle; illness; a broken heart or any number of others – these issues will arise along the way, perhaps a number of times. This is where your healing begins.

For magic to work it must go into your deepest self and the very fabric of the universe. This cannot occur when difficult or painful areas are avoided. It is within those exact places of your suffering that the greatest powers of healing and insight lie and where some of the strongest magic is forged. Each woman experiences this type of inner confrontation and transformation as she journeys through *Aphrodite's Magic*.

It's possible you will come across issues or unresolved feelings too big to deal with on your own. In this case you may need or choose to seek counseling. It's also possible you're already involved in some healing work. By taking responsibility for your well-being and finding whatever support you need, you are able to live your life in fullness and beauty. We belong to a species that works best in groups, loves communicating and has many of its most transformative moments in connection with other humans. Learning to reach out for help and support is a vital part of healing.

The following section includes a short introduction on how to work magic; advice on supporting yourself as you move through the book; materials you'll need and ways to structure a timeline for completing your spell. You can complete *Aphrodite's Magic* in a weekend, work on it once a month for seven months (perhaps on a new moon or full moon) or fit it in whenever you have the time or inclination. You can choose to do *Aphrodite's Magic* on your own or with other women.

Most items for the rituals and processes are easily come by, from nature and ordinary household supplies. You can supplement these with colored or scented candles, with specially bought amulets or Altar cloths, but it's not required. Some things are necessary: A journal and pen; a way to listen to music; uninterrupted time to do the processes and the seven cords themselves; all of which are discussed fully in the Practical Guidelines.

The essential things needed to create Aphrodite's Magic are your commitment, your intention and your willingness to trust in the process. Along the way you will develop your relationship with the Goddess and your own self. Like Aphrodite, you will come to understand and revel in your sexuality, your unique embodiment of the feminine, your beauty and your freedom.

Aphrodite has been a divine Goddess to work with. Under her

guidance I have healed many of my sexual wounds and stepped bravely beyond my past. I have become a Priestess in her Temple and I have witnessed the dances of many other women, as they celebrate and heal their sexuality. I have danced on my own and I have dared to enter a sacred relationship where I am committed to the truth of my sexuality. Part of the dance with my own girdle is this book, which I send out to the world.

Aphrodite's Magic is a magical spell. I offer it to the Goddess, to the women of this earth and the earth herself for the celebration and healing of women's sexuality. Each time another woman enters the Temple, dances to the Goddess and weaves her girdle, the ripples will be felt wherever the feminine is yet to be held sacred.

I invite you to go forth into the dance of Aphrodite. It's time to enter the Temple.

Weave your magic!

JANE MEREDITH

I've realized that I've always regarded myself only as whole, sexual, feminine, beautiful *when I was with a man, never on my own... that I have to reclaim my being 'whole unto myself' in order to love myself. This was a real awakening that came to me gradually.*
  Miriam

BEFORE YOU BEGIN: PRACTICAL GUIDELINES

THE THREADS OF APHRODITE'S MAGIC

My Girdle is very brightly colored, much more so than I would have predicted and whenever I look at it (it is on my Altar) it lifts my heart and makes me feel sensual and sexy. I am looking forward to wearing it for my new friend and I will know when the time is right.

Helen

Here are the practical guidelines to undertake *Aphrodite's Magic*; materials you'll need, notes on how to support this work and optional timelines. If you are about to begin the spell of *Aphrodite's Magic*, read through this chapter before you start and refer back to it as you need. If you're not intending to start the spell just yet, you can browse through this chapter or come back to it later on.

This book and its activities may seem at times to ask a lot of you. They don't cost a lot of money and they're not particularly difficult – but they do take time and space; two things most of us are surprisingly short of and frequently unwilling to dedicate to ourselves. Setting aside time for yourself is a healthy, mature and necessary part of being an individual. Healing and gaining deeper understanding of yourself can only benefit your relationships, your life and your spiritual path.

Celebrating and healing your sexuality and making magical spells take time. They don't consistently happen unless you choose to make them important. If you've picked up this book – if you own this book – then something in you is calling out to make those choices and create the necessary time. What will make it easier is that it's a joyous, revelatory and dynamic experience!

I sensed that my sexuality was too hidden, too shy and undemon-
strative. I was perhaps forgetting the colorfulness of my sexuality.
Change has been subtle too; but I notice I am wearing stronger, clearer
colors and I have taken clothes that hang round me, rather than fit, to
the charity shop! So my curves are more evident and, although I have
not changed in shape, I am enjoying my body shape and form more and
more.
    Kate

Making Magic

Magic is made up of intention, focus and enactment.

There's also an indefinable fourth element – perhaps *magic*
itself. This element has been described as glimpsing the patterns
of the universe. It can be a sudden experience of going *with* the
river of life, or receiving the assistance of the gods. Intention,
focus and enactment are all within your control but this fourth
part comes with grace, when it will, unexpectedly and
undeniably. You can make this fourth part possible by the
strength of your *intention*, you can court it with the clarity of
your *focus* and make room for it through your steady *enactment*.

Intention is just that; what you intend. Often our intentions are
unclear or contradictory and – even worse – they are not always
truly our own. This is why a great deal of attention is given in
magic to working out and declaring your intent; so the magic
you make truly reflects your deepest wishes, best interests and
healthy and reverent self.

Intentions can be pure thought, they may be written down,
they can be spoken – or sung – aloud and they can turn into
whole poems and dances. Intentions are vital to fix at the
beginning of a ritual or magical process and they may need
attention later, as they change, develop or gain a new angle.

Time spent thinking about and setting your intention is never
wasted, even if it takes three times longer than you thought it
would; even if it takes ten times longer. A well-known phrase

within magic is *Intent is All*. Certainly intent is a great deal of magic. Don't skimp on it.

Focus is vital to effective magic. If you're practicing magic whilst trying to write an essay, thinking about tomorrow's schedule or wondering if your new love will ever call you – expect a half-hearted result.

Because many of us find it difficult to hold our focus fully on one thing for any length of time (even minutes), magical spells often have several tracks to them; different ways to claim your attention but all aimed towards the development of the spell. Sometimes these come in graduated steps where the focus deepens one step at a time – smudge the room; cast a circle; dedicate your Altar; do a breathing practice; meditate – and sometimes they all play out at once; such as when you are listening to music, chanting a mantra under your breath and making something with your hands. (Smudge sticks are small bundles of dried aromatic herbs or leaves, either made or bought. When lit at one end they smolder, releasing a smoke believed to be cleansing and purifying.)

Support your focus by not attempting magic when you are overly tired, hungry or distracted. Allow the focus to build gradually, return to it if you get distracted and assist it in every way you can. Meditation is a great tool for building focus and there are many, many books and courses that teach different styles of meditation.

Enactment means actually doing it. So if you read this book from cover to cover, had a strong intention and good focus but actually did none of the processes or rituals and did not have any cords to weave into a Girdle at the end, you wouldn't be enacting *Aphrodite's Magic*.

Enactment means doing it when you think it's silly, when you're sick of it, when you're frightened by it and when you have no idea where it's taking you. It means making the Altar, writing in a Journal, getting the cords that will become the basis of your

Girdle and doing the work.

Magic is not a form of psychological counseling – although both can change our experience of reality and even reality itself – the emphasis in magic is on enacting the mystery, not on understanding it. Some of what you do you may not understand until afterwards; some of it may never make sense to you. Different parts of the enactment will be strongest for different women, so look at your own outcomes to make judgments. Are you healing your own sexuality, or moving towards healing it? Are you celebrating your self, your body, your sensuality and femininity or moving towards celebrating it? In that case keep going, keep enacting.

Within, around and beside *intent*, *focus* and *enactment* you may occasionally feel *magic*. This might be like finding you are suddenly holding the threads of the universe in your hands. It may seem as if you hear the voices of the gods, singing your name. It might come as a sudden rightness, when things shift into alignment and startling clarity. It may be a formless sense of being gifted; standing utterly in the present moment or understanding the purpose of your life.

These moments are transcendent and usually enough to change a life. They add enormous depth and power to your magic. They come when they will. They go, as well; leaving your intent, focus and enactment to continue; enriched, informed and blessed. The results of this process we call *magic*.

Guidelines to Support this Work
Creating and Maintaining Ritual Space

It's best if you have one place you can dedicate to be a Temple space for this work. It needs to be somewhere you feel safe, can easily and happily spend time and can keep some of your things. It can be your bedroom, the living room when no one else is in it, a garden or sheltered outside place.

This Temple will house your Altar – which is described in

detail in the next chapter – and will be where you do ritual, dancing and personal processes, including writing in your Journal. It will be the place where you connect with the Goddess and your inner self. At times when you are not doing this work it may become a living room, bedroom or garden again, but when you take out this book, open your Journal, put on dance music or light the candle on your Altar, it is transformed back to your Temple space.

Your Temple becomes part of Aphrodite's Temple because of your intention and your actions. The Temple can be moved around if you want or need to do different processes in different places. You can move it symbolically – by taking an item from your Altar to the new place – or just energetically and with intention.

Respect for the Depths
This book is not written as a therapeutic tool but as a magical spell. However, the strongest issues you have ever dealt with in regards to your sexuality, your body and your womanhood are bound to arise. These may be familiar to you and need no more than your respect as you touch on them, but they may require re-visiting in depth, to create deeper understanding and resolution. *Aphrodite's Magic* may also open up new areas of grief, pain and uncertainty. There are different ways to deal with this; one possibility is to take time out from this work and its processes to find healing for an unresolved issue.

Aphrodite's Magic invites you to celebrate and heal your own sexuality and is designed to take you wherever you need to go, to achieve that. It may well be challenging. Some places you need to go can be painful. Unlocking and releasing this pain is an essential step in creating your magic and moving towards healing and celebration.

Be wise in it. If you need support, find support. If you need knowledge or healing practices beyond what you can provide yourself, find them. There are many options for healing. Read books; talk to people; find support groups; do the healing work. Seek out massages; dance classes; herbs; therapy or whatever you need.

Be inspired to take charge of your own healing. The woman who wears Aphrodite's Girdle makes her life in magical process and is not disabled by memories, circumstances or fears. Make sure you provide what is best for you at this time.

Taking the Extra Step

The *extra step* is what happens when you come as far as you have ever come before – and decide to continue.

Maybe you have thought about it, but never set up an Altar before. Possibly you have read self help, or magical books but never done the exercises or followed the instructions. Perhaps you long to make things with your hands – or are terrified of it – and don't do it. Maybe dancing is your extra step, or keeping a Journal.

The *extra step* happens when you feel blocked – that you cannot do this thing, do not know how to do it or do not want to do it – and you do it anyway. You take a step out of your comfort zone, out of your safe place and this takes you into the territory where things change; you step into magic.

As you work through *Aphrodite's Magic* you will meet at least one place – perhaps many places – that call upon you to take an extra step. You might not take that extra step every time, or immediately. But you can learn to do it. Practice taking extra steps. Make that spell, write the truth in your Journal (or whatever it may be) joyously, knowing you are stepping beyond your previous boundaries and entering new realms. Tell yourself, *this is the extra step*. Be proud of taking it.

There has been a greater – and increasingly so – love of my whole body
– a pride in it – and I don't think it's any coincidence – I have – for the

first time in my adult life (I am now forty-seven) a wonderful sexual relationship – my body has been woken – I did not believe that was possible, saw myself as a Sex Avoider (beyond the first few months of every new relationship) – something so subtle was celebrated over the weekend of Aphrodite's Magic – It was a coming out of kinds for me.
Catriona

Listening to Your Own Voice
Throughout the book I've placed quotes by women who've done this process, who've worked through the Seven Strands and created their own Aphrodite's Girdle. These quotes are in the book to inspire and inform you; to show the differences of other women and their sameness. They are not meant to dictate your own experience or suggest the correct way of thinking about any process or outcome. These women have widely different backgrounds from each other; including their ages, location, sexual orientation and life situation. What they have in common is they have completed *Aphrodite's Magic* and are willing to share some of their thoughts and experiences with you.

The strongest and most persistent voice in this book is mine. If you don't agree with something I've written, or even something I'm telling you to do; that's fine. My voice offers instructions, guidance, parts of my own journey and some of my understandings about different aspects of women's sexuality. Use it to inform you, inspire you, react against and most importantly, to find your own voice within. What you think, how you feel and the understandings you form are the vital outcome of *Aphrodite's Magic*.

It's possible you will hear judgmental voices as you work through this book; voices telling you sex and bodies are bad, wrong or dirty; voices telling you this is pointless, self-indulgent or even evil. Ask those voices where they come from. Who do they speak for and what is their motivation? You might like to write down what they say in your Journal and then examine it. Ask yourself if you wish to live according to these words. Ask for your own deepest truth. Write it down on the page and fine tune the process of listening for your *own* inner voice.

You might also hear the voice of the Goddess; occasionally, once only or all the time. This could be the voice of Aphrodite, of another Goddess you work with, or of a Goddess beyond all names. Her voice may sound like your mother, a friend or wise teacher's voice. It may sound like your own voice. It may be unearthly or not even speak in recognized words. Usually the voice of the Goddess speaks what we know in our deepest selves. It is most often a moving, magical and transcendent moment. But not always. Again, you can record what is spoken to you and ask yourself for your own deepest truth. If the Goddess speaks to you, respect her words and still continue to search for your own voice.

My Girdle consists of seven colored strands each about two meters in length. These strands have been plaited and decorated with beads, pearls, dried flowers and ribbon. I keep it in my bedroom on my Altar when I'm not wearing it or using it for ritual. I love wearing my Girdle and take every opportunity to do so. It invokes a special sense of womanhood for me when I feel the slight pressure of it around my waist. I walk taller and with purpose and confidence when I wear my Girdle. I feel sensual, lovable and delicious – irresistible...
Tanna

Materials You Will Need
Six different colored cords

The length of each cord is twice-and-a-half around your waist, loosely fitted. (The plaiting process at the end reduces the overall length of the finished Girdle.) The First Cord is colored either gold or silver and the colors of the other cords are chosen *after* or *during* the process for each cord. None of these cords can be red – which is the color of the Sixth Cord – but you can have pink or burgundy.

Either buy cords in a variety of colors to choose from, or wait and buy each cord after you know what its color should be. The colors of the cords are important, so *don't* just buy six nice colors and try to fit them into the process. The results can be surprising – but never unwelcome.

The cords should be lacing cord or twisted cord, not so thick that they will be difficult to plait together, and not too narrow, or your Girdle will have no width. I use cords of about 3mm width, a little thicker would be okay. The cords can be slightly different widths and types from each other – I often use a mix of synthetic and cotton cords, for example, and some are narrower, flatter or have a different look than others. Some variation actually adds to the overall look of the final Girdle.

Red wool for the Sixth Cord
I use bright red wool. You will need between 15 – 30 meters of it, depending on the size of your waist. Specific instructions are in the Sixth Cord chapter.

Sewing things and decorations for the completed Girdle
Decorations are optional and include: Bells, beads, feathers, shells and old jewelry. More on this in the Weaving Aphrodite's Magic chapter at the end of the book.

Journal and pen
This Journal will be the record of all that you do and should be a blank book you don't use for anything else. You can choose an exercise book, a special-purpose Journal with quality paper or make your own book and bind it with a special cover. Choose a pen and keep it with the Journal.

A box or small table for an Altar and things to put on the Altar
You can place magical tools on your Altar; statuettes of the Goddess; drawings; poems; photos; shells and special stones; a

candle; fresh flowers or whatever you like. The creation of this Altar is covered in depth in the next chapter.

Extra bits and pieces from time to time
Various processes and rituals call for different ingredients. These are mostly inexpensive or readily available from any park, back garden or general household supplies. More expensive or beautiful things can be substituted. At every point you choose what will go into your magic and as long as it has meaning and relevance to you, it's fine.

My Girdle is very beautiful. I have added crystals, feathers and flowers to it. It sits on my mirror so that I can see it everyday. I haven't had the opportunity to wear it yet but just looking at it is enough to remember my irresistibility!!!
Shelley

Dancing and Music

There's a lot of dancing in the seven processes that make up Aphrodite's Magic. This is because Aphrodite's Magic is about celebrating both body and spirt, and dancing is one of the most direct ways to access the relationship between these parts of yourself. Aphrodite is a sensual Goddess and dancing is the ideal medium to find your own link to her; further, dance has long been recognized as a path of worship. There are traditions still alive today where priestesses and priests dance as a form of prayer and devotion. Dancing is also a direct experience of being in the body that you can do alone, almost anywhere and in your own style.

The music you dance to will be your choice, although at various points I suggest a mood or tempo. Using a wide variety of different music will give you a chance to experience different aspects of yourself and your relationship to your body. You can borrow CDs or download music as well as using music you are familiar with. Try tribal drumbeats; techno, Eastern or belly-dancing music; New Age chill-out music; single instrument such as flute or guitar; classical, jazz or blues; world music and popular. Listen to this music on a CD player, MP3, your computer or even the radio. Sometimes you might choose to create your own music, either as you dance or prior to dancing; on a drum, rattle or other instrument; or even dance in silence or to music in your head. If you enjoy finding and selecting music, you can put a lot of thought and attention into choosing the best tracks for different processes. Otherwise you can grab whatever comes to hand or seems best in the moment.

If you find dancing difficult for any reason try simply listening to the music and moving just one piece of your body at a time. Try closing your eyes to dance. Or you can coax yourself into it, bit by bit and track by track. Let the music lure you. Let your heartbeat, the pulse beat of your blood, the in and out of your breath tempt you to try moving, flowing, dancing. Let your body come alive.

There is no right and wrong way to dance and it may be one of your challenges to find pleasure in moving your body to music. Your size/weight/age/looks/lack of co-ordination or rhythm are not important. Your willingness to be embodied, to be within your body is crucial. Dancing will anchor your magic into and within your body. It will mean the Girdle you create has your relationship to your body and sexuality woven into it. Dancing is one of the essences of this magic, so it is worth learning to trust yourself in it.

Timelines

The following is a guideline for getting through this book in a particular length of time. If you prefer to wander at your own pace, doing a cord in one day and then taking a month over the next one – do that. If you are working with other women, plan your timelines together.

To Complete *Aphrodite's Magic* in a Weekend:
- Read through and prepare as much as possible beforehand, especially gathering materials and organizing music.
- Begin on Friday night with reading the Invitation and Practical Guidelines. Do all the preparatory exercises in the First Cord and the First Cord itself.
- On Saturday complete the Second, Third and Fourth Cords and on Saturday evening complete the Fifth Cord.
- On Sunday complete the Sixth and Seventh Cords in the morning. In the afternoon do the Weaving and any decorating of your Girdle as well as the celebratory dance.

To Complete *Aphrodite's Magic* in a Week:
- Each day do as many of the preparatory exercises as practical for each cord. Make sure to write in your Journal every day.
- On the first day read the Invitation and Practical Guidelines. Do all the preparatory exercises in the First Cord and the First Cord itself. Begin work on the Second Cord.
- On the second day, complete the Second and Third Cords.
- On the third day, do the Fourth Cord.
- On the fourth day, do the Fifth Cord.
- On the fifth day, do the Sixth Cord.
- On the sixth day, do the Seventh Cord.
- On the seventh day do the Weaving, decorating of the Girdle and celebratory dance.

To Complete *Aphrodite's Magic* in a Moon Cycle:
- On or just after the full moon read the Prologue and Practical Guidelines. Gather your materials and your music.
- On or around the waning, half-moon complete the First

and Second Cords.

- On (or just before) the dark moon, complete the Third and Fourth Cords.
- On or around the new moon, complete the Fifth Cord.
- On or around the waxing, half-moon, complete the Sixth and Seventh Cords.
- On the next full moon do the Weaving, decoration of the Girdle and celebratory dance.

To Complete *Aphrodite's Magic* in Seven Months (Seven Moon Cycles):

- Complete one Cord per month, including the further exercises listed after the Cord work.
- Continue writing in your Journal throughout each month.
- Explore the Resources for each Cord in the month of that Cord.
- In the final month – as well as the Seventh Cord – do the Weaving, decoration of the Girdle and celebratory dance.

If you prefer to complete *Aphrodite's Magic* in your own time:

- Do as many of the preparatory exercises for each Cord as you can.
- Continue to write in your Journal, even if you are 'in-between' Cords.
- Set aside clear, specific times for the main work of each Cord.
- You can do the exercises at the end of each chapter as you feel to, including over-lapping as you move on to the next Cord. Explore the Resources at your leisure.
- Do encourage yourself to complete the whole process; for example set a goal to complete it within a year. A half-made magical Girdle is not half as effective as a completed Girdle; it is not a Girdle at all. Enlist the support of others, of your innermost self and of the Goddess if you feel

yourself flagging.

It has pink, red, green, silver, black, yellow and Bordeaux (wine color) cords and two small mascots, but I am still working on it. I wear it in rituals that I think will need Aphrodite's influence. I keep it on or near my home Altar, usually framing the big round mirror behind the Altar. Wearing the Girdle connects me to the ritual power of women. It reminds me of the women's rituals I have been in and of this important manifestation of Goddess power that women's bodies are.

Berin

FIRST STRAND: THE GODDESS

I did know Aphrodite before, but dancing with her made me feel that beauty and strength do go together, that receiving and giving cannot be separated.
Miriam

Aphrodite is a Goddess from ancient Greek mythology who embodies love and beauty. She is associated with the sea, sexuality, dolphins and the power of love. Often she is depicted as naked or nearly naked. She has a role in many myths, but it is as she appears in Botticelli's painting of her birth from the ocean that she is most remembered. In this famous image she looks directly at the viewer as she steps to shore from a scallop shell, naked but for her hair. She offers herself and is also contained in herself. She appears as a divine archetype, a sympathetic mentor and a role model for radiant, self-possessed femininity.

A Personal Goddess

There are some experiences I think of as my Aphrodite moments.

Once I stood naked on a deserted beach at 11pm under a full moon, absorbing air and light and asking my life to turn with the turning of the moon. In that moment I felt completely whole.

Distraught, I have entrusted myself to the waves, sobbing and pleading with the sea for healing. I was enfolded by the ocean's cleansing force, washed clean of history and pain. She cradled me on her waves, born again.

When my child was small I sat in shallow waves with him, delighted with their splash. We waded and skipped over the incoming tide. Once we saw a wall of fish swim through the face of an uplifted wave. We've watched dolphins playing so close we felt we could reach out and touch them.

I've built sand-mermaids with groups of women, diving

seaward as we decorated their hair with shells and seaweed. I've stood on the rocky edges of cliffs under spray, watching waves crash and seen the ever-changing beauty of the world in those drops of water. I've seen silver moon-paths stripe across the sea, inviting impossible adventure, and at the Winter Solstice I've stood on cold sand and watched the sun rise, orange-gold from limpid, metal-grey water.

One winter full moon night I was in a women's circle on the beach. We had a fire. A woman we didn't know walked by and asked if she might join in. There was a gap in the circle, where the smoke had been blowing. She stood in that gap and we said "yes". When we began the ritual, she spoke her part as if she had long worked with us. She sang when we sang, the songs we always sang. She knew the words. When we began to call to the moon she took her clothes off (we were wearing jeans, boots, jumpers and coats but she had on only a sarong) and walked naked around the fire, her arms uplifted to the moon's light. At the end of the circle she left, saying she was a traveler and did not have a telephone number.

When my son was three I took him to a Beltaine ritual. We danced outside, under the moon's light. He danced by himself and when I came up to him he said, breathless: "The Goddess is dancing here! Can't you see her?" I looked and saw only moonlight, the shadows of trees; I felt the breeze. But I'm sure she was there.

Aphrodite is with me all the time. Even though the Valkyrie in me often takes over, Aphrodite reminds me that people deserve a chance, specially me! And that I need to be sweet, open, loving and accept the love of others… even if it's not all perfect – they also have to learn. Aphrodite guides my way and makes me peaceful. I feel much better.
Artemesia

Who is the Goddess?

The Goddess is a historic – and pre-historic – figure. She has many names and many faces, stretching further back in time than we have written records. The generative life force of the feminine has been celebrated as divine in countless ways in countless cultures.

Between these Goddesses all aspects of life are embodied: Birth, maidenhood and innocence; pregnancy, lactation, fertility and motherhood; death, dying and the afterlife; justice, wisdom and initiation; love, beauty and sexuality. She has been known as the earth itself; as the night sky; the sun; the moon; the evening star and as numerous named deities throughout history. Aphrodite is one of these many Goddesses.

The Goddess is also seen as Gaia, the literal embodiment of the earth and all its beings, and as an alternative – or equal – face of God/the divine/Oneness. She is often depicted as an animal or bird and has a long and ancient association with trees, pre-dating the Druids' sacred groves. In current times deep ecology, eco-feminism and environmental activism all embrace the concept that the earth is not inanimate, separate from us or merely our domain to use how we will, but rather a unity of which we are all a part.

Many women relate to *goddess* as an integral part of themselves; the sacred thread that holds them to life, their inner knowing or an expression of their spirit. They may choose various Goddesses to honor, to journey with for a while or dedicate themselves to but that particular Goddess – be it Indian Kali, Sumerian Inanna, the Christian Mary or Egyptian Isis – is rarely their complete experience of *goddess*. Rather, to choose (or be chosen by) one of these faces of the Goddess is to approach her more intimately. By honoring one facet of Goddess we can move closer to the whole.

I think it was the first time I really worked at developing a relationship with Aphrodite at all... It was not easy to go from the dark into the light, from warring and mistrust to honoring the sacred body. But I think it was worth it. Aphrodite has become a little bit more present in my life... I don't know if I will ever be able to fully embrace her and honor her as I should... but she has given a new name to another strong power that has always been part, however hidden and encapsuled, of my life: unconditional and unbounded love.

Berin

Aphrodite as Goddess

Goddess of love, beauty, fertility and sexual rapture – Aphrodite's reputation stretched far beyond her Grecian origins. In the Roman pantheon she was known as Venus and she has links to even older Goddesses. Like Babylonian Ishtar and Sumerian Inanna she is associated with the morning and evening star (the planet we still call Venus). In the modern world her name is one of the relatively few Goddess names still familiar to us.

The most well-known version of Aphrodite's birth is written by Hesiod, an early Greek poet who lived around 700BC. He wrote a tale of the Titans, the ancient race who came before the Greek Gods we know of today. One of these Titans, Kronos, castrated his father in a bid for power. He threw the severed genitals into the ocean, whereby Aphrodite was conceived. She emerged from the sea as a fully mature Goddess.

This is the image we are familiar with from Botticelli's painting, *The Birth of Venus*. In the last week I've noticed a print of that painting on the wall of my physiotherapist's office, as well as a line drawing of it in a newspaper (advertising cosmetic treatment for veins). A friend has a lamp with that image printed over it and I have notepaper that uses it as a watermark. Aphrodite's image and associations have survived and adapted.

Aphrodite's Girdle

In the older stories Aphrodite is unmarried and freely takes lovers amongst both Gods and mortals. The God of Love, Eros (also known as Cupid) is said to be her child by Ares (Mars), the God of War. In other stories Aphrodite's husband is the smith God, Hephaestus, who makes gorgeous adornments and weapons for the Gods.

One of the smith's most famous gifts to Aphrodite was a magical Girdle that represented her intrinsic qualities. Woven from precious metals, it conferred irresistible sexual attraction on the wearer. Occasionally Aphrodite loaned this Girdle out to others. Hera, Queen of the Greek Gods, used it to distract her husband, Zeus, during a crucial moment in the Trojan War, thus enabling the Greeks (her favored side) to overpower Troy. The war itself was supposedly over the possession of Helen, a mortal woman with her own Goddess-like beauty.

Aphrodite's Girdle influenced more than the outcome of wars. Quite ordinary women might be expected to be familiar with it. Plutarch, a Roman historian who lived in the first century wrote in his *Advice to the Bride and Groom*: "Thus a lawful wedded wife is invincible if she has everything in herself – dowry, birth, potions, Aphrodite's magic belt – and wins goodwill by her character and virtue." (*Advice to the Bride and Groom*, translated by Donald Russell.)

Aphrodite is one of the Goddesses who is still called on today for assistance in matters of love and passion. Her Girdle – with its middle-Eastern associations of belly-dancing, sensuality and seduction – is a symbol that continues to resonate with us. Her proud ownership of her sexuality inspires women to make their own choices, respect their bodies and honor the deep feminine.

Approaching Goddess

The following activities will assist you to begin Aphrodite's Magic.

The Goddess Within

Time: 30 minutes
You will need: A Journal devoted to your work with this book

Leave the front page of your Journal blank for now and begin on the second page.

Write down the following headings, one per page. Write your answers under each heading. You may wish to write more later, as you continue your journey.

- What does the Goddess mean to me?
- Do I carry the Goddess within me? How/Where?
- What activities could I do to honor the Goddess?
- What are my feelings and thoughts about Aphrodite?
- How could I strengthen the Aphrodite aspect of myself – and what would happen if I did?

Casting a Circle and Raising Energy

Time: Initially 30 minutes. Subsequently 5-10 minutes each time you work with this book.
You will need:
- Optional magical tools such as candles, incense, rattle
- Optional cord or chalk to mark out your circle

The work for each of the seven cords that make up Aphrodite's Girdle begins with casting a circle, raising energy and attending to your Aphrodite Altar (instructions for creating an Altar follow this section).

Casting a circle and raising energy are essential preliminaries to magical work. There is no single, or correct, way to do these things – only different ways. Suggestions follow and the idea is to find what works for you – which might be listed here, may be whatever you have been doing for years or can be something you've just thought of.

You might prefer to cast a circle and raise energy the same way every time, feeling that repetition builds up the magic and assists the mind to slip into a magical zone – or you might prefer to change things, so each time it is slightly different, appropriate to the work you intend to do, your mood and the time available. There is no right and wrong way.

The point of casting a circle is to declare (primarily to oneself, but also to the spirit and practical worlds) that now is a time you have set aside for magic, ritual and personal process that cannot be interrupted or minimized. Raising energy is used to gather all parts of yourself into focusing and deepening your presence, awareness and power.

At the end of a ritual or circle we 'ground' the energy, which is a way of coming back to current reality, as well as dispersing excess energy into the earth as an offering, gift or cleansing. This is an important step. Skipping it can result in symptoms such as dizziness, exhaustion, extreme openness and vulnerability and an inability to return to normal (unmagical) functioning.

To Cast a Circle Do One or More of the Following:

- Determine the compass directions, East, South, West and North; or if you prefer, South-East, North-East, North-West and South-West. Mark out the directions with candles, rattling or drumming or calling to each direction. Visualize the four points as stations guarding your circle.
- Beginning either at your Altar or in the East, walk slowly and carefully around your circle; heading South if you are in the Northern Hemisphere, North if you are in the Southern Hemisphere. You are following the direction of the sun and moon as they travel through the sky. You can carry a magical tool, smudge stick, rattle or drum if you like. Visualize yourself as creating a strong boundary between the inside of your circle and the outside.

- Sit or stand quietly in front of your Altar and visualize a dome of sparkling, starlight energy that stretches over your head and under your body to encompass your whole circle.
- Take a long ribbon, rope or cord and place it carefully in a large circle around yourself, with your Altar either inside the circle or as part of the boundary of the circle.
- Follow a method in a book that describes circle casting in detail.

To Raise Energy, Do One or More of the Following:

- Stand or sit inside your circle and drum, rattle, tone or chant, calling upon spirit and/or the Goddess. Begin softly and continue until the call is very strong and regular – stop at the height of it.
- Establish your connection with the earth and/or the heavens. Imagine yourself drawing upon that earthy/celestial energy and pulling threads of it into yourself. Feel yourself slowly filling with this energy and stop as you reach the peak of it.
- Put on music and dance until your whole body vibrates with your heartbeat.
- Follow a method in a book that describes energy raising in detail.

To Ground Energy, Do One or More of the Following:

- Sit or crouch quietly in your circle with your palms down to the floor/ground and imagine all the excess energy leaving your body through your hands and feet and returning to the earth.
- Close down the circle you cast by doing in reverse order whatever you did to cast it (gathering up your ribbon,

walking backwards around the circle) whilst all the time mentally dispersing the circle energy and sending it back into the earth.

- Blow out all candles, thank the Goddess for her presence and acknowledge her within yourself. Stamp your feet hard on the ground several times and say "The circle is complete (or grounded)."
- Follow a method in a book that describes grounding energy in detail.

Practice casting a circle and raising (and then grounding) energy until you have a method that works for you.

Creating an Aphrodite Altar
Time: 30 minutes to an hour
You will need:
- A box, shelf or small table for your Altar
- An Altar cloth
- Items for the Altar
- An image or symbol of the Goddess

The Altar you create for Aphrodite will be the symbolic centre of your magic. It can be an Altar you construct and then take down for every session but it's easier if you can create your Altar and then leave it for the length of this work. It is possible to have a moveable Altar – on top of a small table for instance – that you may keep in your bedroom or study most of the time, but move into a larger space when you are actually working with it.

Choose a practical place to create your Aphrodite Altar – the centre of the living room is probably no good but against one wall, or on top of a bookshelf may be fine. The Altar should be in the room where you plan to do most of the work of this book – which includes dancing, writing in your Journal and various rituals and processes. You may even want two Altars; one outside (especially if you have a fountain, stream or pond nearby) and one inside where you can do most of your work and safely leave your Journal and the cords of your Girdle as you gather them.

You can add to your Altar and take things away from it anytime. Everything on the Altar reflects your personality, your intention, your offerings to the Goddess and your own process. You can re-do the whole Altar at any stage in your process – what is important about it is that it reflects you and your connection to the divine. It may start very simply with a colored cloth, a single candle and a handful of shells and progress to holding all sorts of spells, notes and pictures. It may change with every one of the processes you work though, or with the seasons or it may remain consistent throughout, with a fresh flower to replace an old one the only visible change.

Begin with a cloth over your Altar. Cloths can be: A scarf; fabric from an old-but-loved piece of clothing; a specially-bought piece of velvet; a small table-cloth or embroidered runner. Wrapping paper is a nice alternative.

Then choose a centerpiece. A candle is often used for this, or a small vase with a single flower, or some kind of statuette or representation of the Goddess. Be aware that burning candles on your Altar usually results in spilt wax at some stage. It's also a fire hazard, so never leave lit candles unattended. Blow them out and relight them when you return. You may choose instead to have a photo of yourself in the centre, or some of the decorations you plan to put on your finished Girdle. You don't have to have a centerpiece at all, or you can leave it empty until the right thing turns up.

Place some items on the Altar which you feel represent your connection to Aphrodite and your hopes or plans for this magical work of celebrating and healing your sexuality. These might include: A special pen to write in your Journal and the Journal itself; shells, seedpods or particular stones; crystals or feathers; a hand-mirror; a picture, photo or drawing of the sea or the

Goddess; a few tools such as incense or smudge stick; chalice (maybe filled with sea-water) and scented oils. Underneath the Altar, or nearby, you can keep matches or a lighter; spare candles and incense; colored pens and pencils; rattles, chimes or a drum; a cushion and shawl; a box of tissues and anything else you think you might need.

I really appreciated the initial visualization in Aphrodite's Temple – I still have a very clear and detailed picture of what it all looked like and now and again I go to the Altar and have a little dance with Aphrodite!
Gini

Dedication
Time: 15 – 30 minutes
You will need:
- Your Aphrodite Altar
- Your Journal and pen

Your dedication is a crucial part of this First Cord and your whole Aphrodite's Girdle. The dedication should sum up in a sentence what you are offering or asking of yourself or the Goddess as you do this work. Write it in your Journal, speak it in front of your Altar, keep a track of any changes to it as you move through the work and always remember that *intention is (nearly) everything*.

Begin by casting a circle and raising energy, as described above. Meditate for a while in front of your Altar and let your intention arrive – it is not always what you assumed it would be nor does it always make immediate sense, but it should feel right to you. If it is very complex, try to simplify it so it can be easily expressed. Some sample dedications follow:

- *I dedicate this work to finding my freedom as a woman.*
- *I offer my heart, my vulnerability and my trust to the Goddess.*
- *I dedicate myself to love.*

- *I ask Aphrodite, Goddess of Love, to heal my fear and pain.*
- *I offer my uncertainty and my willingness.*

To make your dedication light the candle on your Altar (or incense or smudge); or sprinkle a few drops of water from the chalice over the Altar and maybe over yourself. Acknowledge the presence of Aphrodite in her symbols, picture or figurine. Then speak, whisper or sing your dedication, looking at the Altar. Spend some time simply near the Altar, either meditating, dancing or writing in your Journal. Once you feel complete remember to ground your energy, as described above, close down the circle and extinguish any candles and incense or smudge.

Looking for Aphrodite

Where do you think the Goddess of Love might be found? At the beach? In your bedroom? Under the full moon? At a dance? Maybe in the pages of a poetry book?

In your Journal make a list of places you might find Aphrodite, either as a force outside yourself or as an inner experience. Go to some of these places, with Aphrodite in your mind. Take her an offering (always natural and bio-degradable if you plan to leave it there, such as fresh water, a feather, flower or special rock) and spend some time feeling out the qualities of the place and waiting to sense Aphrodite's energy. Take your Journal with you and record your impressions in words or drawings; go for a walk (or a swim); chant – aloud or under your breath – or perform one of your rituals or processes.

Look for Aphrodite in yourself. Look for moments of unbridled delight in your body, whether it be achieving that yoga stretch; brushing your hair; putting on your new jeans; admiring the competence of your hands or making love. Be aware of those moments when you get a rush, or a tingling of excitement, awareness and entrancement. You might choose to borrow some of Aphrodite's unabashed delight in her sensual self or ask her to assist you to lose unhealthy habits. Let her confidence ripple through you, dare your edges in dancing, in creating poetry or art and rip aside your veils in disclosing the truths of your heart.

I had forgotten how wonderful it is to dance. I think that went a long way to opening up the Goddess within. And I had also forgotten how erotic/sensual dancing could be...
Shelley

Invoking Aphrodite

Perhaps you've looked for Aphrodite and can't find her? Any quality you wish to have in your life can be invoked – called in energetically – so you begin to act like a magnet (or creatrix) for it. If you decide to invoke Aphrodite you should be specific in exactly what you are inviting into your life – remember she is the Goddess of love and beauty, sexuality and sensuality! So be precise. Don't put out a general call for lovers unless you are ready for the result. A specific invocation enables you to be discriminating, so you can fine tune particular aspects of the Goddess you wish to incorporate into your life.

It is unethical to ever name someone else in a magical act without their clear consent. Ask for *the right lover* or *someone who truly appreciates me* or *a partner I can love with my whole heart* rather than using a name. Even if you are already in a partnership, try to make your invocations primarily about yourself.

Some samples invocations are:

- *Aphrodite – help me love and accept my whole self.*
- *I call on Aphrodite, sea-born Goddess, to enable me to enjoy my physical body.*
- *Goddess Aphrodite, please teach me to see you in myself and other women.*

- *Guide me, Aphrodite, to move towards a truly loving and equal partnership.*

You can invoke Aphrodite at your Altar, at the sea or any natural water source or wherever you feel she may be found... whether that be the mountains, a forest, your backyard or your bed.

Aphrodite is my favorite Goddess and being Greek myself I am deeply connected to her energy. I love her unapologetic sense of power, her entitlement to pleasure and resistance to patriarchal restraints. She has the power of feminine beauty, something that men at least have envied or feared and tried to control over the centuries. She is these days the Goddess whom every woman needs to claim...
Golden

Preparation for the First Cord
Time: Allow an hour, which includes time for dancing and Journal writing
For the First Cord you will need:
- Your Aphrodite Altar, which may include a candle, incense, smudge stick or chalice
- Your Journal and pen
- Your First Cord. This should be silver or gold. Its length should be two and a half times around your waist, loosely measured. More details about the cords can be found in the Practical Guidelines. If it is the kind of cord that frays, knot both ends. Coil it up and place it near you while you do the visualization.
- If you think you will be cold, have a shawl or blanket to wrap around you
- Music to dance to – choose music that is both solemn and uplifting – it can be Eastern, belly-dancing music; it can be a piece of Western Classical music or some kind of devotional prayer/trance or dance music. It should last for

at least ten minutes and it's good to have a second track you can continue dancing to, should you feel like it.

- You might also like to have some very soft, meditation-style music playing throughout your visualization. This cuts out the distraction of background noises and surrounds your inner journey within a cocoon of appropriate sound. I use music which sounds like it might have been played in ancient Temples. If you choose to do this, make sure you can change to your dance music quickly and easily.
- The Guided Journey. You can pre-record the guided journey (visualization) in order to play it back to yourself. You can have someone else sitting with you for this part of the work (or for all of it) and have them read the journey to you; if they are doing the work as well, you can take turns reading it to each other. Another option is to read it through several times before beginning your visualization and then, closing your eyes, take yourself through as much of the journey as you remember. Yet another option is to list the main points of the journey (having read through it several times); *back through time, gardens, temple...* on a card which you keep in front of you as a prompt (you can look at it if you forget what comes next).

I felt I was transported through time and space to a place beyond this world and there was within me purpose, surrender, safety, reverence, service, holiness...
Tanna

The First Cord: The Goddess
This is the central work of this chapter.

Begin at your Altar. Light a candle, sprinkle a few drops of water, or light the smudge or incense. Remind yourself of your dedication. Sit or stand quietly before the Altar until your mind settles and you are ready to begin.

Cast a circle that will hold you energetically through the whole time. You can call to the directions (North, East, South and West) if you like, and/or invoke the elements of Earth, Air, Fire and Water. If you prefer, you can draw a circle around the room with a magical tool or your hand. Visualize your circle as containing you comfortably and safely. You can invoke an energy or presence that you feel will offer you guidance and protection. Also ask Aphrodite (or the Goddess) to be present.

Choose an appropriate way to raise energy; chanting, meditating, drumming and dancing are some of the possible ways. Allow your energy to fill your circle, bathe the Altar and enliven your whole body. You can use an energy raising technique you are familiar with, or create a new one just for your Aphrodite work.

Now sit comfortably upright; cross-legged or on a chair. Close your eyes and begin focusing on your breath. If you are accustomed to meditation you can follow your own method of relaxation. Otherwise spend some time relaxing, so your breath comes slowly, deeply and regularly.

Once this is happening become aware of each part of your body in turn, sending your breath towards it and reminding that part to relax. In this way move through your toes, feet, ankles, calves, knees, thighs and gradually up the body, remembering to release any tension held in each place. Include the pelvic area, stomach and chest as well as all the limbs, neck, scalp and each part of the face and mouth.

Re-establish your slow, deep breathing if you have forgotten it during the relaxation. Then ground yourself by connecting strongly with the chair, floor or cushion (whatever you are sitting on) and underneath that, the earth. Feel your connection to the realm of earth, the here/now and the solid, physical fact of your body. Take a few breaths feeling your body's gravitation to the earth.

Now turn your mind to the visualization, beginning by imagining yourself slipping back through time.

This guided journey is the magical action of the First Cord, so bring all of your intent and focus to it.

Guided Journey

Leave your body here and imagine yourself slipping backwards through time... take your spirit-self back through time... back through your own time and then back through your mother's time; back through the time of your grandmothers; the time of your great-grandmothers and the time of your great-great-grandmothers...

Back and back you go, back through time until you reach the place beyond time...

You feel it gathering around you, the time of the Temples... You are entering into the time when great Temples stood in the cities, when the Temples were the centre of civilization, when the Goddess was worshipped through all the lands. In the time of the Temples priestesses were honored, the rites of the Goddess were kept and people lived in harmony with the earth, sun and moon. You have sent your spirit-self back to this vast, mythical time and you feel the threads of it gathering around you...

You arrive at the edge of a garden that encircles one of the Temples. Find your feet there and look around you. You see the gardens stretching out before you and in the distance, the roofs of the Temple. Look around at the gardens. Admire them – the trees, the flowers; maybe you see herb beds or vegetables growing. The sights and scents of the garden are all around you as you begin walking towards the Temple. You might smell freshly turned earth, or sun-baked clay, or rain; you might smell perfumes, spices or compost. Listen to the sounds you hear as you walk; maybe there is the sound of children playing or women talking quietly, maybe you can hear singing or music or birds; maybe there's the sound of running water or a wind blowing through the garden.

Look at the path under your feet and notice – is it trodden earth, a paved path or a soft carpet of moss? Does it wind about or does it head straight for the Temple? Perhaps it is geometric rather than curving, skirting different garden beds. Use all of your senses to imbibe the full beauty of this Temple garden.

Then you come to the steps of the Temple... Notice how they have been built, how they are shaped... And now look at the Temple itself, the main doorway and what you can see inside.

Take the steps that lead to the Temple and stand in the doorway for a moment. Again, use all of your senses – smell, sight, hearing, touch and even taste; open your mouth and taste the air of this Temple. Now walk into the Temple. Feel how it feels in your body, to be walking into this place.

Notice the shapes of the building. Are there Altars? Windows? Pillars? Paintings? Statues? Other women? Perhaps there are candles and incense, or pools and fountains; perhaps there are comfortable places to sit or small gatherings of women; perhaps there are children playing.

After you look around the main Temple you see a doorway you had not noticed until now – and you realize this doorway leads to the innermost Temple of Aphrodite. You have never been inside it before, but now, today, you suddenly feel ready to enter this innermost sanctum – and now you go through the doorway and enter this sacred place.

Once you are inside, make an offering to Aphrodite – perhaps a strand of your hair, a piece of your jewelry or a flower you brought in from the gardens. And then dance, dance for Aphrodite before her Altar, in her innermost Temple. Close your eyes and ask for her to come to you, in your dance. Explain your need to her, your desire, your longing... Repeat your dedication here, listen to it resound off the walls and echo through your being. Call her to you.

And go deeper – into your deepest heart – and call to her from there – and dance as strongly as you can... Offer yourself to her...

And she comes to you... Aphrodite appears. And you know immediately she is the Goddess. One moment she is veiled and one moment naked... you see she wears a silver and golden Girdle, draped about her hips... she is your mirror and all that you aspire to be and she is more than any human; she is the Goddess and she takes you up. She dances with you.

And there is never enough time in this magical space, but she has come to you, she has seen you, you have felt her, known her presence...

And she takes from her belt, her Girdle, a single strand; the finest thread of silver, of gold, of starlight, of aether and she hands it to you... and in your hands it becomes solid, thicker, a material thing fixed in time... and you hold onto it as your gift from her...

And before she goes, she offers you a blessing; she whispers a word, just one single word into your ear, and then she is gone...

And you take the strand, the thread from her Girdle and you leave this innermost Temple and go back to the main Temple... and you find a place to sit and just to be... you stay quietly for a while...

Now you need to return, to leave the Temple and go back through the gardens, back to the edge of the garden where you arrived. Walk slowly, appreciating all the sights, smells and sounds of the garden and this whole sense of the Temple, of the time of the Temples and this Temple in particular. When you reach the edge of the garden, still holding tight to the thread from Aphrodite's Girdle, let yourself slip once again into the time stream, now heading back to your own time.

You feel yourself leaving the time of the Temples... You are moving through time again, through the time of your ancestors; then the time of your great-great-grandmothers; of your great-grandmothers; of your grandmothers; your mother's time and then back to your own time, your own place, your Altar and your body sitting there, waiting for you to return. Return. Return.

When you return, take up the silver or gold cord you measured beforehand. This is the thread from Aphrodite and it is the first strand of your own girdle. Name this First Cord with a single word. It can be the word Aphrodite whispered to you, or else her name *Aphrodite*.

Put on your dance music and dance, with your First Cord, to Aphrodite. Remember your earlier dance, within the Temple and let this dance of your body reflect that dance. You can dance renewing your dedication, your thanks or your request to the Goddess. Dance for the full ten minutes of music, or longer if you choose, stretching and moving your body in recognition and thanks of its connection to your spirit and the Goddess.

After dancing spend some time recording your experiences in your Journal, including the name of your First Cord.

Remember when you finish to close down the circle you cast, grounding yourself and the energy. This is an important part of magic and a way to come back to yourself and ordinary life. Read the notes earlier in the chapter for ideas on how to do this. Do remember to put out any candles you've lit before you leave your Altar.

The Silver Cord reminds me of the bright, still moon power of the Goddess, but also of the cool power of a blade... There was a strong flow of dark warrior and crow energy in me that clashed with the creative, loving power... And I must admit that I have only recently – almost one year later! – started to understand what kind of power this could be and how I can connect to it in a new and personal way... The dancing was great. I love dancing. After all, the warrior and the crow have their dances too. It helps me to transform fight energy into creativity.
  Berin

Developing Relationship with Goddess
These are optional activities. They can be done after you have completed your First Cord or at any time during the remainder of your work with this book.

Maintaining Aphrodite's Altar
Throughout the time you are working with this book, continue to

pay attention to your Altar.

Different ways to do this include: Daily placing a fresh flower on the Altar; lighting a candle for at least a few minutes each day; doing a daily practice, such as yoga, meditation or Journal writing in front of your Altar (you may choose to dedicate this practice to Aphrodite); adding new things to the Altar as you find them – shells; your cords as you gather them; any other spells or charms that you make; poems you write or pictures you draw.

Sometimes you might want to re-make your Altar to emphasize a completely different aspect of Aphrodite or yourself. For example, you may initially have created the Altar to represent a sea-like Aphrodite, with a blue cloth, many shells, a goblet of sea water and a blue candle. Now you feel the sexual and sensual side of yourself stirring and to support and celebrate this, you remake the Altar with a red or pink theme, including a drawing or statuette of Aphrodite wearing a Girdle, low on her hips or some of your favorite jewelry. Or you may have begun with a very nurturing, great-Goddess style of Altar, with a bowl of earth, crystals and photos of people you love and feel like moving into a much more playful place, refreshing your Altar with a mask, belly-dancing chain and a deck of Tarot or Goddess cards.

Perhaps you prefer your Altar to be a pristine place with only a candle, or a single representation of the Goddess. This is fine. It is really the intentions that go with the Altar, and your mindfulness that give it power, not the number of objects you place on it or how often you change it around. Different styles suit different people; whereas one woman might make her Altar in the living room, another may have it tucked away on a shelf in her bedroom and yet another may have it in a grotto in the garden.

I did call on Aphrodite since... went back to the Temple and talked to her, listened to her. It really was an experiment in trusting, and my faith in her has grown tremendously since then. I feel now I can call on her and trust her concerning my love life, and also I do not feel anymore that she'll make me submissive or that I'll lose my freedom if I'm to be in a relationship.

Diane

Your Journal's Title Page

Decide what you would like on the front page of your Journal. Perhaps it is a prayer or poem to Aphrodite, perhaps your dedication, an illustration of Aphrodite or a scene from nature.

Decorate your title page near your Altar, with music playing and a candle burning. Afterwards, leave your Journal on or near the Altar to ask the blessing of Aphrodite as you continue this work.

Aphrodite Research

There are a number of books that include sections on Aphrodite, as well as several books that name her in the title, following her theme of love and sexuality. There are also many books of mythology – world mythology, or Greek mythology – that include stories of Aphrodite amongst other Gods and Goddesses. The internet is another rich source of stories, theories and personal reflections.

Follow the threads that appeal to you. You may be interested in researching the myths told about Aphrodite, the Grecian culture she came from or a modern uptake, such as contemporary women's and girls' relationships to their bodies and sexuality.

Resources

- *Aphrodite's Temple: Guided Journeys* (CD), Jane Meredith. www.janemeredith.com
- Botticelli's painting of Aphrodite is held at the Uffizi Gallery in Florence, Italy and can be viewed online at: www.virtualuffizi.com/uffizi1/Uffizi_Pictures.asp? Contatore=25
- *Conversations with the Goddesses: Revealing the Divine Power within You*, Agapi Stassinopoulos. Stewart, Tabori & Chang, 1999
- *Goddess: Myths of the Female Divine*, David Leeming and Jake Page. Oxford University Press, 1996
- *New Larousse Encyclopedia of Mythology*, Robert Graves. Crescent, 1987
- *The Goddess Within: A Guide to the Eternal Myths that Shape Women's Lives*, Roger J. Woolger and Jennifer Barker Woolger. Ballantine Books, 1989
- *The Red Book: A Deliciously Unorthodox Approach to Igniting Your Divine Spark*, Sera Beak. Jossey-Bass, 2006
- *The Spiral Dance: A Rebirth of the Ancient Religion of the Goddess: 20th Anniversary Edition*, Starhawk. HarperOne, 1999

SECOND STRAND: EYE OF BEAUTY

The beauty of the other women present repeatedly brought tears to my eyes and it completely changed the way I see the women around me now – looking beyond the surface and feeling for their real selves, the specialness.

Miriam

What do your eyes find beautiful? A forest? Waves breaking on a beach or a night sky? A new-born baby or a group of children playing a game together? A bowl of cherries? A magazine model, or the clothes she wears? Your sister, mother or grandmother? Yourself?

Are you beautiful on a good day, dressed to go out in flattering clothes, conscious of the eyes that will look at you? Or are you beautiful with unbrushed hair, dressed for warmth or practicality? Are you beautiful at night, getting ready for bed?

Have you ever looked in the mirror when you've been crying for hours? Once I took close-up photos of a friend who was crying uncontrollably. We were at the beach on an overcast day and she was tearing a relationship out of her heart. They are powerful photos; I think she was startled by their beauty. Her whole being is there in the pictures; deep, vulnerable and alive.

The Moment I Became Beautiful

I was nineteen and with a group of women in the changing room of a public swimming pool. One of the women, many years older than myself, was riveting and sensual. She came over to me and gripped me by the elbows so I could not escape. She gazed into my eyes and said with utter conviction, "You are so beautiful". And I understood that I was. In the eyes of a woman I had been named beautiful. I had never considered that of myself before. I knew I was attractive, intelligent, insightful; many things, but beauty had never been on the list.

In my mid-teens there was a pre-occupation amongst the girls I knew. The question that raged was: *If you could be rich or beautiful or intelligent, which would you choose?*

Of those three things, beauty was the most vexed. Rich was obviously crass, intelligence was obviously necessary. We couldn't afford to choose beauty, not really, because to put beauty as a primary value was to instantly categorize our lives as obsessed with appearance and we knew that wouldn't be enough. Yet how we desired it. To be beautiful.

We tried to gamble with these choices: Perhaps if you were beautiful, you could marry someone rich and intelligence wouldn't matter so much? Or if you were rich you could somehow buy beauty and intelligence? Maybe if you were intelligent nothing else mattered? And we all, admit it or not, wanted to be beautiful – someone the world smiled upon just for her looks, before she had to prove herself with tests of character, application, originality and values. Intelligence was admirable, wealth was practical but beauty was the most desirable. We longed for it.

The crime of this was it did not occur to any of us (however intelligent) that we were, already, beautiful in our fourteen, fifteen, sixteen year-old selves. We were healthy, had for the most part clear eyes and skin; we were fit and lively; we smiled and laughed with ease; we were beautiful. We were also intelligent; we were the girls with good marks, with friends, ambitions, a lively interest in life and the world and we were, in many ways, rich. We lived in middle-class suburbs, in the affluent first world with parents who had jobs and owned a house; we had clothes, food, shelter, education and no reason not to go to university or get a job on leaving school and create financial security for ourselves.

Why did we confine ourselves to that question, which we asked endlessly? Why did it not occur to us we could have beauty, intelligence *and* wealth, or indeed, that we already had them? It is only now, in my forties, I can say with confidence; well I am and always have been intelligent; I am, in my own way, beautiful and I am, to all effects and purposes, rich. If those things still matter to me – I have them.

I can't think, now, what it would have taken to believe in our own beauty. Those who the rest of us considered beautiful seemed truly to doubt themselves; to be eternally nervous about their appearance and ridicule anyone who suggested their prettiness. I can't believe it was all put on. Just as the rest of us didn't know our generic beauty of youth and promise, they did not know their individual beauty.

There is something women do that I'm trying to understand. Because the ideals we are presented with are so impossible to achieve (a starving teenager whose body type only represents about five per cent of the population, as Diane Sylvan so charmingly suggests in *The Body Sacred*) it often seems even those attributes we do happen to have (shiny hair, smooth skin, a slender waist or luscious breasts) are not good enough for us. So a woman with long legs will sigh and say she is dumpy with large thighs – I think genuinely believing this – but then her friends, listening to her are thrown into comparison, because none of *their* legs are nearly as long or slender as hers, so now they all feel awful. If even her legs are not beautiful, what hope do any of them have?

I've experienced this as a woman with thin friends. Once I sat with three women and listened as one by one they spoke about diets and how desperate they were to get rid of the fat they were carrying. This wasn't at high school; this was in a Goddess circle with women in their thirties who were creative, successful and gifted. They had children, relationships, jobs they loved. None of them were – even remotely – fat. I, on the other hand, was distinctly fatter than them and not on any diet. I did not consider myself unbeautiful, or even overweight. I felt increasingly uncomfortable as the conversation continued – were they expecting me to participate? Were they even deliberately pointing out my excess flesh, especially compared to them? Were they just utterly blind?

I've listened to women rave enviously about my breasts. "Look at my whole body," I say. "Look at the rest of my body as well," – to have them fall uncomfortably silent. Or when I have pointed out to thin women, bemoaning their weight, who they are speaking to (aren't their eyes working?) they say, "Oh, on you it looks wonderful, you are Rubenesque/delicious/sensual. But on me it would be awful," – with no apparent irony.

I'm sure most women have had experiences like this, tailored to our own sensitivities and insecurities. Doubting your own beauty seems to occur regardless of the particularities of your body. It makes up part of what being a woman is, in our world.

Don't you wonder what it was like in the times of the Goddess temples?

It was like, do you really mean that? Do I really look good? It was strange yet good. It was beautiful! It's not that I lacked self esteem it's just that I'd managed to put so many protective layers over my vision of myself... I realized it wasn't the outside world judging me. It was my own judgments on myself that were causing me insecurities.

Artemesia

Behind the Eye of Beauty

Many fairy tales have beauty as one of their key ingredients and I don't think it's co-incidence. There's Sleeping Beauty (who was cursed and nearly died because of her beauty); the Snow Queen whose terrible other-worldly beauty steals away a young man; the warning tale of Red Shoes where vanity destroys the spirit and eventually the life of a young girl and many others.

Diana Wynne Jones' *Howl's Moving Castle* is a modern twist on this beauty story, with the protagonist spending nearly the whole story in an eighty year-old body, instead of her own eighteen year-old body. Despite this, she is able to win the respect and love of her 'prince', the wizard Howl, proving that physical beauty is not everything.

There's also an old story about one of the knights of Arthur's Round Table marrying an ancient hag as a matter of honor. She then confronts him with the choice of her being a hag by day and a beautiful maiden at night, or a beautiful maiden by day (when others will see her) and a hag at night (when he will be alone with her). His gallant answer, that the choice must be her own, breaks the enchantment and she resumes her true shape of a beautiful maiden, both night and day. We are left to infer that his detachment from her beauty is what saved her; that he gave more regard to her as a person than he did to either his own pleasure or his status regarding her beauty.

In this world we receive far more negative feedback about women's bodies than we do positive. It can be hard to cling to a belief that we are beautiful just in our womanhood and our unique expression of that; hard to believe we shouldn't be on a diet, wouldn't look better in new clothes, weren't born too tall/short, could do without color in our hair.

However good our self-image is, however sincerely appreciative our lover, friends and family are, it's always out there – cellulite warnings, teenage glamour models, endless advertisements for cosmetics, air-brushed bodies of the famous – and the exaltation of youth, youth, youth. If it was age that was valued we would have some hope; that's where we are all incrementally heading and we could show off signs of progressive aging easily – smile lines, silver hair, stretch marks from babies – but as it is youth that is valued, it appears we are all doomed.

A friend of mine in her fifties, in a radical attempt to age gracefully, purged her nearly waist-length hair that she had dyed black since she was a teenager. She cut it off, stripping back the color in stages over several months to finally arrive at her own gentle silver hair, just long enough to frame her face. The irony is now other women keep asking her where she got her color done, because not only does it look wonderful, but amazingly natural! (Amazing!) It was done in the beauty parlor of the Goddess.

If beauty is in the eye of the beholder, what does it take to see someone as beautiful? To see the effort they have made to present themselves to the world, even when they do not meet our own aesthetic standards? To admire their natural attributes, whether they be strong legs, curly hair, graceful hands, clear eyes? To be able to gaze upon their soul in some way? To see their essential self revealed? It's an interesting concept, because it takes the emphasis of beauty away from the *subject* of the eye and places it on the eye itself. The one looking becomes responsible for finding beauty, rather than the one looked upon responsible for providing it.

Even more than our consciousness around the eyes of others judging us, firstly and absolutely, it is our own eyes. If you don't recognize your beauty when you look into the mirror – and I don't mean the beauty of your clothing, make-up or hair cut – then it seems obvious no one else will be able to convince you of your beauty. If you only see the clothes you have chosen, make-up you have applied or your hair cut/color/style, your understanding of your beauty will be eternally limited to those items. You will only ever see yourself as beautiful according to your accessories.

Ah, but it's in the eye, the eye of the beholder; your own eye. Learn to behold yourself as beautiful and you allow others to see that also.

About my appreciation of women's bodies, I can only say: "Come on! I'm a dyke! I've always been and will remain inspired by women's bodies (and not only in a sexual way, à propos)!"… What can straight women – the full impact of whose femininity is often undervalued by their partners – teach me about appreciating women's bodies? (I don't mean to be offensive, but at this point I really believe being a lesbian is an advantage).

Berin

Approaching the Eye of Beauty

These activities are the lead-in to the Second Cord. Do both of them if you can.

We have been raised in societies where beauty is measured against external, usually unobtainable models of femininity; ideals that have been constructed from abstracts rather than real women. Even super-models – who represent a very tiny proportion of our population, being both very young, very tall and very thin for their height – are not left to rest in peace having attained such beauty, but continually critiqued for any sign of aging or obvious flesh. Knowing we can never look like those women does not place us outside the realms of striving for this unobtainable badge. And aging – any kind of aging; into your twenties, never mind forties, sixties or eighties – only takes you further from the ever-elusive goal.

If you regard yourself as beautiful in spite of all this, you are a lucky and empowered woman. Perhaps – like me – you came early into an understanding that beauty rested in the unique existence of an individual, not any collection of attributes. Perhaps you have trained your eye over the years to gaze on your humanity; the way your face shows wisdom, intelligence, high spirits or the way your body is open to life and at ease with itself. Perhaps you have the words of a loved one – parent, lover or friend – to whisper to yourself as you gaze in the mirror.

You will spend time cultivating your eye to appreciate beauty as you move into the Second Cord of Aphrodite's Girdle – your own beauty and the beauty of other women – the individual beauty of each one of us and each part of us.

The Beauty Parlor of the Goddess
Time: 10 – 30 minutes
You will need:

- Your Journal and pen
- Colored pens or pastels

On a new page in your Journal either draw or write an answer to the following question:

What were you handed out in the beauty parlor of the Goddess?

Try to view yourself *not* as a series of omissions or negatives. Rather, catalogue your favorite parts of yourself; your best features, whether they be quirky and individual, classically beautiful, sexy, refined or elegant.

You might go further and list or draw parts of yourself that you can appreciate even if they have never been aesthetically admired – I'm quite short but have strong, sturdy swimmer's legs – I've always thought of them as my worst feature because they are far from slender or long – but in fact they've been good to me. You may have features you get from your mother, father or racial type that you can appreciate as a visible sign of your heredity. Perhaps there are details so tiny no-one else would ever notice them – the fingernail that was torn off when I was ten years old regrew as the strongest and most shapely of all my fingernails.

At the bottom of the page – or around the edges – write a decorative *thank you* to the Goddess for your personal beauty.

Opening the Beauty Eye
Time: Short periods of time over several days
You will need:

- Your Journal and pen
- As needed: Massage oil, music to dance to, camera or drawing tools, sewing or jewelry-making things...

Step One

Choose just one piece of your body that you like: A hand, a breast, an eye, an ankle... and do three things to show your appreciation of it (this can be over a few days). You might draw it beautifully in your Journal, or photograph it and paste in the photo. You can bathe it; anoint it; massage it; decorate it; buy or make it a new piece of clothing or jewelry; write a poem for it or perform a special dance based entirely around celebrating that chosen part of your body. After you have done three things keep coming back to that part, looking at it again, gazing until your gaze softens and you see the beauty of it and feel your appreciation flowing through you. Record your activities and responses in your Journal.

Step Two

Now choose a part of your body you feel more dubious about – maybe your thighs, nose, hair or feet. Once again, undertake three activities which involve appreciating that part. If you have a lover, you might ask for special notice to be given to that part of you, to add to your own appreciation. Attempt to arrive, over a few days, at a place of admiration for this part of you that has had so little praise or positive attention. You might admire its practicality; its simple existence as a part of your body in this amazing life; its potential when it receives some praise... In your Journal record your appreciation activities and your responses.

Step Three

Now choose a part of yourself you have criticized, wished was different or have tried (or even managed) to change. Some part you judge too big or small, too hairy or the wrong color. Maybe it is something you keep hidden all the time, even from yourself or maybe it's a part you constantly flagellate, metaphorically or literally beating it up, trying to make it different. Go for appreciation. You know how – belly dancing, push-up bras, gentle massage by candlelight after a bath... You can do it. Three things. Record your activities and your feelings; note any changes in your attitudes in your Journal.

Preparation for the Second Cord

Time: One to one and a half hours, but this may need to be broken up into sections.

For the Second Cord you will need:

- A variety of other women to look at, in an extended gazing kind of way. You can ask your friends to sit for you, or choose women in cafes, trains, waiting rooms or parks (anywhere you can find them).

There is no requirement at all about these women – they can be any age, any style, any color, weight or look. If you are picking strangers, you might like to deliberately choose women you ordinarily wouldn't look at, women who don't seem remarkable, glamorous or exciting.

For this work you're asked to choose three different women. If you find the process especially difficult or confronting you can practice first, looking at a whole variety of women and choosing one beautiful thing about them. Continue looking at each woman who crosses your path or your vision, until you can see one distinctly beautiful thing about each one. It will not always be the first thing that caught your eye, or what you expected – it could be a much older woman has a sensual beauty you wouldn't ordinarily look for, or a classically attractive woman may, as you gaze at her, actually appear defensive or brittle and you have to look deeper to find her true beauty.

- For the final part of the process you will need either a friend (or another woman doing this process) or else a large mirror – one your whole body can be easily seen in.
- Your Journal and pen

- The Second Cord – the color is chosen *during* the process, so do not choose the color of this cord *before* the process. Arrange this in a practical way for yourself – either have a variety of colors to choose from, or wait until the color is chosen and buy the cord afterwards.
- A clock or watch with a minute hand
- Dancing music

I do recall a lovely feeling of sisterhood and profound joy in seeing the beauty of another woman without having to feel threatened or envious.
Golden

The Second Cord: Beauty
This is the central work of this chapter.

You can do this cord work over a number of sessions, in one session, or over one day. If you are working by yourself, use your Journal for automatic writing. Automatic writing means you do not edit (even in your head) what you write as you go along. Keep writing fast and continuously for the set time or set number of pages. Do not give yourself time to reflect and don't worry if you're repeating yourself or your sentences are ungrammatical. Automatic writing is an attempt to access the more creative and spontaneous parts of the brain, as well as genuine emotions and responses.

If you are working with someone else use a large clock with a minute hand that can be easily seen. If you are working alone you can use a wrist watch laid out on your Journal.

Read through the whole section before you begin.

It was difficult at first, but very beautiful after, to let myself be touched by many little different details I found beautiful in a person that I didn't find particularly beautiful or attractive.
Diane

Choose Your First Woman

If you are looking at strangers, sit somewhere you can observe people without seeming to stare too much. If you are working with a friend, your responses will be spoken instead of written and you can stare as much as you like.

Observe this woman. Look at her individual, unique beauty and either speak it out loud (to your friend) or write it down (if it is a stranger). If you are speaking, speak for two minutes continuously, without pausing. If you are writing, write for either five minutes or two pages.

Try to focus not just on listing her beauty – *great hair, nice face, friendly smile* – but give descriptions of it, including how it makes you feel, for example: *Great hair, there's an element of wildness there, I can see how it springs out from your head and brings a real aliveness to your face; the skin of your face looks really soft and gentle and your eyes hold a lot of depth and compassion in them; friendly smile, the corners of your mouth turn up in a way that makes me imagine a laugh is just below the surface.*

Talk, or write, not just about the face of the woman you see in front of you, but her whole body; her posture and attitudes; her movement if she moves while you are studying her; her choice of clothing or presentation of herself.

If you are talking to a woman sitting in front of you, try to make it a continuous two minutes of talk, with no gaps at all. Sometimes this means repeating yourself but you will usually find new details or explanations to add. These two minutes are an extraordinary gift to give someone, so fill your time with as many details and personal observations as you can.

Choose Your Second Woman

Again write or speak, depending on whether you are working with someone you know or looking at a stranger. This time, look not just at her individual beauty as a woman, but also look for the Goddess within her. Sometimes you will see this in her posture, her hand movements or in the way she holds her head; if you are sitting close to her you will almost always find it in her eyes, if you look for it. When you find it, make a note of it (or speak it aloud), *I see the Goddess in you*. Then continue detailing aspects of her beauty for the set time.

Choose Your Third Woman
This time record or speak the exact nature of the Goddess you see within her beauty – it may be a dancing Goddess, a forest Goddess or a mother or grandmother Goddess; it may be a Goddess who is fierce and wild, or one of ultimate compassion and understanding. Try to describe how you have seen the Goddess within this woman – is it the shapes of her body and face, the light in her eyes, the clothes she has chosen to wear? Add as many details as you can in your time.

This was a very emotional and deep exercise – I did it with someone I have known for a little while and felt instinctively close to and it deepened our relationship and was very self affirming. I can still remember her words.
  Helen

You are the Fourth Woman
Even if you have worked on your own, looking at strangers up until now, you may choose to have someone else work with you for this last part. If you are alone, gaze into the mirror. It is no less powerful – possibly more powerful – if you are confident you will be able to look at yourself the same way as you have looked at the other three women you have studied.

Understanding your own beauty makes the magic of the Second Cord, so bring all of your intent and focus to it.

If you are working with someone else it is your turn to sit silently whilst she details your beauty to you, aloud and for two minutes. Either demonstrate beforehand (on her) or explain carefully what you want her to do. It's important she speak continually for the whole two minutes and she describes your unique beauty to you, as she sees and experiences it. Ask her also to look for the Goddess within you and to describe something of how that appears to her.

Immediately at the end of the process ask her what color she feels best compliments your particular beauty – and this is the color for your Second Cord. Don't worry if it's a completely different color than the one you would have chosen – perhaps you always choose blues and purples, yet she has chosen brown for your earthy humor and sensuality – honor her vision of you and your beauty in the color of the cord.

If you are working alone sit before the mirror so you can see your whole body – either arrange the mirror and yourself on the floor, or sit on a chair before it. Gaze at yourself in the mirror until you reach a state of inner calm; let your eyes rest on their reflection. When you are ready take up your Journal and pen and, giving yourself the same time or number of pages as you did the first three women, describe your beauty on the page.

Remember not to pause or edit, or worry if the sentences are incomplete or ungrammatical. You are reaching for something far deeper. Notice things you have never noticed before; look as if you were a stranger at this woman in the mirror. Search for the Goddess within and describe her nature if you can. At the end of your time or when you have reached your prescribed length of writing, lay the pen down and gaze once more into your own eyes. Take a moment to really acknowledge the beauty you have just seen.

You have a stillness and deep sadness in your eyes that seem to hold unending compassion. You have a vulnerability around the eyes, as if you will receive each hurt as it comes. The folds of skin over your eyelids have this delicate, delicate skin. Your hair is rich and natural and full of life, with glimpses of age and mystery. You hold tears just behind your eyes; your eyes shine with other-worldly beauty. Your skin is smooth and pale and inviting of touch, of stroking and smoothing. The lift of your head is courageous.

Your beauty is that of a woman receiving life and waiting – asking to be moved by it. You have a lop-sided beauty of the left side being much more expressive than the right. You have an aliveness, a mobility of features and expression. The beauty of your eyes is of presence, awe and knowledge, shining – love and hurt battle equally in your eyes. There are beautiful curves between brow and eye and curl of hair and cheekbone; there is a peacefulness in your face at rest.

Your eyes shine. Luminous.

Jenny

Now choose a color you feel most compliments the exact nature of the beauty you have been studying and recording. It will rarely be a color you wear a lot of, it may be a color you wouldn't wear and yet it reflects this particular beauty. That is the color of your Second Cord.

Jane chose for me a brilliant puce, pink cord and it gave me deep surprise and pleasure. I was surprised she saw this brilliance in me and I found myself struggling to accept it, but longing to do so. I realize, looking back, that I now wear quite a lot of this and very similar colors, all new to my wardrobe. Wow! I hadn't noticed, until asked, how much this had impacted on my sense of Kate, and my enjoyment of Kate!

Kate

Choose a name for this second cord from the words spoken to you, or that you have written, describing your beauty. It should be a single word – such as *vivid* or *serene* or *luminous*. If no word springs to mind, you can name the cord *beauty*. If you have cord of the right color available, measure and cut your Second Cord straight away and add it to your First Cord – wherever you are keeping them – under your pillow, on your Altar or wrapped around your waist. Otherwise, buy the cord as soon as possible, in the color that was chosen for you.

When you have your Second Cord do a celebratory dance with it, acknowledging and appreciating your own beauty.

Sum up, in your Journal, where this Second Cord has taken you and the feelings you have explored along the way. Note especially how you now relate to your own beauty and the beauty of other women.

Remember to complete your session with closing down the circle and grounding your energy.

The moments of telling and listening were great gifts, giving me the feeling to be perceived as I really am, with my body and soul. It was not only the words that changed the perception of myself, but also the intense eye contact and wordless closeness of this moment. There was also the amazing feeling to see another woman in depth, seeing into her soul and trying to verbalize what secrets and pearls are hidden under the surface and come to shine in exquisite beauty.

Miriam

Delving Deeper into the Eye of Beauty
These activities are optional. They can be done after you have completed your Second Cord or at any time during the remainder of your work with this book.

Finding True Beauty
Devote a few pages in your Journal to this or else make a larger piece – a poster or mandala – that can be stuck on your wall or become a back-drop for your Altar.

Find images that reflect your appreciation of the true beauty of women, using magazines, your own supply of photos or the internet. You might choose dozens of photos of eyes, for instance, or different stages of women's lives, from little girls through to ancient great-grandmothers. You might choose photos of yourself and your friends, either clothed or nude, or photos of your daughters, nieces and grand-daughters.

Arrange the images in ways pleasing to you. Add drawings, decorations and words if you like. Let your eyes immerse themselves in the images.

If you have young daughters, encourage them to do this process as well.

Gifts for the Goddess

Next time you have to choose a present for another woman – your mother, sister, daughter, friend or co-worker – think carefully about the particularity of her beauty and buy or make something you feel really reflects these qualities. When you give it, express your appreciation of her beauty and explain why you chose that gift and how you feel it reflects her. If you like and it's appropriate, also share with her an aspect of the Goddess you feel she carries.

You can do this with more than one woman!

Wearing Your Beauty

Choose the clothes you are planning to wear for the day to reflect how you wish to feel, not how the world expects to see you. Thus on a day you're feeling truly terrible you can wear your best clothes. Just glancing down at them, let alone feeling them about your body will lift your mood. Maybe you love beautiful underwear – it doesn't matter no one else can see it, just wearing it is a sensuous luxury to remind you that you are a spark of the Goddess. Perhaps you love jeans and boots, or clothes that make you feel practical and invincible.

Wear colors you love – if a color consultant has told you to wear neutral browns and creams but you love orange, pink and purple – I'm pretty sure you'll feel (and even look) better in those bright colors. You can try out variations for fun – a cream dress with a purple belt and pink shoes (well, I would).

Wear jewelry that means something to you. Think of all the associations stored into jewelry – a wedding ring is just one example – and wear items you chose for yourself, or that people you love have given to you, or pieces with magical or ritual significance.

Nurture Your Beauty

Nurture your inner beauty. Consider your resources carefully: Would paying for a manicure give you the most benefit, or a massage? Will those shoes you're considering nurture every step you take?

Hold a non-traditional beauty evening with your girlfriends or women's circle; you can include foot massages; home-made cleansing face masks; henna painting; hair braiding, beading or wrapping and of course a spa-bath or swim if possible. Ask everyone to bring beautiful food and drink and either read poetry or listen to music that is inspiring, uplifting and represents the deep beauty of the soul.

Resources
- *Howl's Moving Castle,* Diana Wynne Jones. HarperCollins, 2008
- *Howl's Moving Castle* (Film), directed by Hayao Miyazaki, 2004
- *Inner Goddess Makeover,* Tanishka. www.starofishtar.com
- *The Beauty Myth: How Images of Beauty Are Used Against Women,* Naomi Wolf. Harper Perennial, 2002
- *The Body Sacred,* Dianne Sylvan. Llewellyn Publications 2005

THIRD STRAND: VOICE OF TRUTH

When I said "I am a real, happy, complete woman, a woman whole unto herself" I was so surprised by the sound of the words that have been unknown to me until this very moment. I have not had the chance to speak the truth about my sexuality since. I have that inner knowing of where my path with my own self-love might lead, but I think I would have to speak the words to make the path manifest. But where? To whom? Who is going to listen?

Miriam

Why is it such a challenge to speak the truth? Surely that's what we've always been taught: Tell the truth. And truth, so the saying goes, is simple.

But it's never simple. There are all those other, conflicting things we've heard as well: *If you can't say something nice, don't say anything at all.* And the persistent belief that no one really wants to hear; that anything we have to say couldn't really be worth listening to, especially if it's just personal, about a problem or doesn't have solid facts to back it up.

Speaking My Layers of Truth

I've always thought of myself as a truthful person. Of course, truth comes in a number of layers. Often it's easy to believe I'm speaking the truth only to realize, later, there was a whole level of emotional truth that didn't even get acknowledged. How much simpler communication would be if we could just say *I'm anxious* or *I'm afraid of losing control* or *this is what I long for* instead of having to couch our speech in rational arguments and logical phrasing.

But it's something else again when you don't even recognize your truth.

My relationships and sexuality have been unconventional for

most of my life. I've always believed in personal responsibility, for all of my actions and all the consequences of my actions, and I've been very reluctant to lay down rules for other people. Although I have strict internal moral codes, from the outside my behavior may look random, dangerous or just plain stupid.

For a long time I refused to dictate any terms or conditions to a lover; or attempt to control any choice or action of theirs. This seemed like the unviolatable truth to me; that they should exercise free choice in their life, unhampered by my wishes, needs or even advice.

Where I came undone in this noble ideal was around the issue of other lovers. I did once – in my twenties – have a good relationship with a loving partner which was successfully an open relationship; that is, we both had other lovers and other relationships during it. I think it was successful because we were very, very good friends; had great communication; a genuine love for each other that was not primarily possessive and were able to process emotion – perhaps we even enjoyed it – whenever it arose.

I extrapolated from this situation to imagine that in my thirties – by now with a child, and wanting and needing quite different things – the same principles applied. I had several extremely painful relationships where I tolerated my partner taking a lover. I stood by my truth at all times – my truth being, it was not up to me to dictate the parameters of someone else's life, choices or relationships. The other truth I had – of pain, distress, absolutely not wanting this and not being able to cope with it – I considered lesser; in fact, I did not even recognize it as a truth. I swept it aside. I did not speak it, I barely thought it.

I was astounded when men I was with lied to me about their involvements with other women. Here was I, so truthful and yet they did not tell me the truth. I could hardly credit it, even the first time; let alone when it happened a few years later with a another man. I said it was all fine, their own choice, nothing to do with me; so why did I feel physically ill, deeply betrayed and emotionally distressed? I said it was because they had lied to me.

I finally learnt my deeper truth; it was my lie that made me ill. The truth is I don't like it when my lover sleeps with someone else. I still don't necessarily think it's wrong, but I don't want to be involved with it. It may have suited me when I was twenty-five, it doesn't any longer.

I still struggle with expressing the truth. I often choose to stay silent if I think what I have to say might not be welcomed and I skate above some of my more ferocious truths, seeking to soften them. But at least I feel I am on a bedrock of knowing my own truth. Sharing it can be more difficult, as all sorts of terrors raise their heads; the fear of displeasing, of being rejected, of having to justify and of being shamed. But I am committed to try.

Background to the Voice of Truth

Truth responds best to acknowledgement. It does not respond well to argument, persuasion, or alternative views. Anything less than acknowledgement diminishes what has been spoken.

Perhaps this is why people are often able to share deep truths in somewhat formal situations, where they do not know the other people very well – a counselor's office, a support group or a workshop of some kind. Their listeners do not seek to correct them with their own knowledge of the situation or the speaker's character and they stay politely silent until the speaker has finished. Whereas when we speak to our families, our partners, our closest friends they have so much invested in their view of our histories and personalities it can seem like a battle to express anything at all outside those parameters.

If you have to consider all the consequences of truth before you speak, the truth rarely gets spoken. This is not to ignore that obviously there are some times and places better suited to deep, revealing speeches than others. But speaking the truth rarely feels safe – it leaves us no place to retreat to. It can be good to get a lot of practice in, whether it is in the aforementioned counselor's office and support group or whether you are able to set up a truth agreement with a friend or partner. You can also practice with yourself; speaking aloud, speaking to the mirror and writing in your Journal.

Truth tends to create a large silence around it. It rarely falls within the rules of social politeness. It is often raw, startling, unapologetic. It draws attention to us. Speaking the truth about difficult and painful things means we will have a lot of attention focused on us, just as we are at our most vulnerable. The truth can challenge long-held beliefs that have been maintained in silence, where certain things are never mentioned. Just naming those issues is incredibly powerful and to speak one's truth about them can be world-shattering.

There are many layers of truth. The level of truth we reveal may be pragmatic, deceptive, partial or obscuring. But most times when we don't tell the truth it is not deliberate manipulation, but simple avoidance. The truth is not always likable and can be perceived as hurtful. What do we do then? Create some level of compromise, where we keep silent; merely imply something we are not willing to say directly; or speak a little of the truth and wait to see how it is received?

I think women have been taught to stay silent. Not that we always follow what we have been taught; but I have met so, so many women whose throats close up as they struggle to speak secrets they have unwillingly held, as they try to find a voice to sing with or a way to express feelings and thoughts they have believed unspeakable. Speaking the truth can appear unattractive but its alternative leaves us imprisoned in fear, lies and pain. Finding the right level of truth-telling is an important part of being true to yourself.

The Truth About Sex

Telling the truth is one thing but telling the truth about sex and sexuality is a whole extra thing. All our vulnerabilities seem to double or triple when it's sex we're discussing. So many fears, old patterns and sub-conscious messages try to get into the conversation. It can sometimes appear impossible to say even the simplest of things, or to actually hear anything your partner is trying to say. Sex itself is so intense, so unworded; I don't even know if it's possible to tell the entire truth about it.

These challenges appear when we first become sexually active and remain throughout our sexual life – to tell the truth about what you want and what you are offering; about what you like and don't like; to truthfully say how you feel... not just once but dozens and probably hundreds of times.

In truth-telling about sex these ordinary challenges are difficult enough. Telling the truth about sexual abuse, things you wish you hadn't done or sexual thoughts your lover may find threatening are even more difficult terrain. These things can be so difficult to express you may wonder why anyone would even try.

Some people and books advocate a system of total truth – to speak each passing thought, so everything is communicated. Others counsel to link wisdom with such sharing, so profound information is communicated but things that are merely hurtful or divisive are not disclosed. Still others advocate that lovers respect each other's separate lives and regard as private anything that does not directly concern the other person.

Each individual and couple makes these choices, which may be revised and rewritten many times. I believe even discussing desired levels of truth leads to more ease with truthfulness. This assists in really difficult areas, where people may long to speak truthfully but don't know how to go about it. A guide I find helpful is a commitment (to oneself, or to a partner) to *either* speak the truth or say, at the time, "I'm having trouble speaking the truth about this". This flagging of difficulty makes more room around the subject matter and the listener generally becomes sympathetic and attentive to what is obviously a sensitive subject. Just acknowledging the difficulty can make it easier to begin speaking the truth.

Recently I met a woman in her seventies. I was startled when she told me, fairly early in the conversation, that she had the best sex of her whole life when she was seventy-four. She said she thought it was really important to let people know good sex isn't confined to a certain age and doesn't end with menopause. The conversation left me in awe. It's a radical approach to truth – to begin a conversation (even with a stranger) with the most important things.

Approaching the Voice of Truth

These activities are the lead-in to the Third Cord. Do as many of them as you can.

Voice Challenges – Singing, Speaking, Chanting

Having a working voice is an essential, though mundane, part of speaking the truth. Three levels of challenges follow, in each of three categories: *Singing, Speaking* and *Chanting*. In each category, take the challenge at the appropriate level for you. If you already sing everyday in the shower, for example, you would have to go to the second or third level to actually be challenged. For each one, record in your Journal the challenge you are choosing and your learning and development with it.

If voice work calls to you particularly strongly you might choose to do more than one of the levels in each challenge, even continuing to work on it after your Girdle is complete.

Singing
Level 1: Sing by yourself; in the car, in the house or on the beach (or anywhere outside). Sing for enjoyment and keep singing until

you like the sound of your voice. Play with sounds, experiment.

Level 2: Go to a group singing event. This could be a place where spiritual or religious songs are sung, or singing for pleasure or a community sing-a-long. Sing at least loudly enough for those next to you to hear your voice. Open your mouth, smile inside your head and send out your voice.

Level 3: Join a choir; take a singing class (group or private); or if you are already a singer, sing solo for a group of friends or at a community event.

Speaking

Level 1: Ring a talkback radio station on a topic you care about; or ask a question at a public forum or raise a concern with a local politician, school headmaster or similar (but verbally – not in writing).

Level 2: Give a short speech or presentation to a small group (political, social, work-related).

Level 3: Be interviewed on local radio or give a talk at your local school or somewhere similar about something you really care about. Join Toastmasters or a drama, improvisation or conversation group.

Chanting

Level 1: Find some chants you like (these can be found on CDs, pagan or Goddess internet sites and some books have chants in them). Practice two or three you like (with a drum or rattle if you have one) until you know the words and tunes.

Level 2: Teach some other people your chosen chants (your kids, a women's group, a small gathering). Teach them the words and then sing with them. This can be a good opener for a lot of different gatherings – it doesn't have to be the main event.

Level 3: Write your own chant. Chant it every day for a month; maybe by your Altar, in nature, as you wake and on going to sleep or to your loved ones. Alternatively, teach and lead a chant to a larger group, as part of a ritual or gathering. Or else join or start a chanting group, where chants are shared and sung together.

Writing Truth

Time: Give yourself a set time of 15 or 20 minutes
You will need: Your Journal and pen

Sitting by yourself with your Journal start writing the truth. Write the truth about yourself, your life, your dreams, fears and pains; the truth underneath the everyday; the truth behind your habits and friendships and loves. Write the truth of your essence, your soul.

You can scrawl. Scribble. Weep as you write. Don't use proper sentences. Write in lists – write big – small – messy – neat – anything. Just write down the truth. As much of it as you possibly can in the time you've given yourself.

At the end of the time, stop. Even if you haven't finished, stop. Even if you've written hardly anything, or nothing at all; stop. If you feel you really haven't got to the truth, or there is more that needs to be expressed, come back to it the next day; but for now, stop.

You might want to read back through what you've written. Or not. That's okay. You can draw a box around your words, a colored border to commemorate: *This is the truth*. However ugly or difficult, however frighteningly simple and powerful and alive, it's the truth – your truth.

Another practice with writing truth is to take a single thought or situation and express your truth concerning it. Then pause and see if you can go deeper with that truth. Continue until you reach a truth which seems complete (often it will be much simpler than where you started).

True to Yourself, True to Others
Time: 30 minutes
You will need: Your Journal and pen

How often do we tell small lies to ourselves? That nothing is wrong, for instance, or we don't care when a friend slights us or no one appreciates the meal we just cooked?

Down one side of a page in your Journal write a list of your most common (or it could be most recent) untruths to yourself. On the other side of the page note down if you are willing to switch to the truth in that situation, and how and when you will do that.

Place the word TRUTH in the centre of a new page. Draw a circle around it; then draw three more circles (progressively bigger) around that. Think of those people – and there may not be any – with whom you would trust the entire truth – about yourself, about your feelings for them, about your dreams and vulnerabilities – and write their names inside the circle with TRUTH written in it.

Then think of people whom you trust most of the truth with, or most of the time; people who, just occasionally, you might protect from your real opinion or the depth of your emotion. Place their names in the next circle, one step removed from TRUTH.

The third circle is for those whom you have a kind of social truth with; you know what's going on in each other's lives, but perhaps you don't probe too deeply; although you feel – at need – you could and would trust each other with the deepest truth.

The fourth circle is for those whom you don't tell the truth to. You protect yourself – or them – from your true feelings and thoughts. You edit yourself and/or you avoid their truth. Write their names in.

Now look at the names in the circles. What strikes you first? Is there anything you wish to change? Are there people you wish you shared more with? Perhaps there is no one you trust with the truth, or you are uncomfortable with anyone at all being in the inner circle? Perhaps you look at those names in the outer circle and wonder why they are in your life at all, or what you are protecting by being so guarded with them?

Make some decisions now about the place of truth in your life and truth in your relationships. Write your decisions down on the next page.

Preparation for the Third Cord

Time: Allow 45 minutes

For the Third Cord you will need:

- Your Aphrodite Altar
- Your Journal and pen
- A cord, ready measured and cut, the color of your choice (to represent your truth)
- The option of a helper/witness or else a mirror
- Make sure you read through the whole process before beginning

This process was very important to me because I needed to be able to say something about incest. I had been in a healing process around the issues linked to it for quite some time, but I needed to state it in a circle, to feel this issue was over and done with. Saying "the truth is I can love and be loved" was also very powerful for me, it was like casting a spell of hope for my love life.

Diane

The Third Cord: Truth

This is the central work of this chapter.

Finding out where we are bound, and unbinding ourselves, is a work in progress. It's hard to imagine women in this age (where so much binding, both literal and metaphoric occurs) might actually get to the end of unbinding. But every ingrained belief – unbound – is another piece of your truth, power and beauty freed up.

You may wish to do this process with another person, a friend, counselor or even your partner. Doing the process with someone else will make it logistically easier; it will also mean you have a witness for the truths you speak. If you choose to do it alone, be aware this cord is about *speaking* (not thinking) and make sure you speak aloud through the process.

Choose a color for the Third Cord, the cord of voicing the truth. Measure the cord to the same length as the others. Cut it and knot the ends.

Prepare for the ritual: Cast a circle, sit in front of your Altar, spend some time chanting or meditating, do the internal preparations you have decided on.

Now begin to think about what was said to you, growing up, about women's sexuality. (This may include things you overheard or inferred, from indirect comments).

Your parents or teachers may have said specific things to you; given you information, warnings or stories of one sort or another about women's bodies, women's desires and women's responsibilities and choices regarding sex. Your friends or older siblings may have told you secrets, jokes or whatever information they had come by; perhaps to prepare you but perhaps to impress or frighten you.

Scan through these different things you heard, noting your body's reaction to each one; for example you may feel a kind of armoring, where your body clenches up and your breath goes shallow.

When you become a teenager usually you are exposed to various forms of media – books, films, magazines, TV and billboard ads – as well as often receiving some instruction at school, perhaps also through religious or social organizations about sex and sexuality. Try to remember the different feelings this information generated in you – maybe curiosity or antici-pation, fear or guilt, uncertainty or confusion.

As soon as you became sexually active a whole new realm of words existed – words said to you specifically about your sexuality, your body and your desires – words spoken by your lover or lovers, your girlfriends, maybe your parents or a doctor or other professional. Recall what was spoken to you and how you felt about those words. Did you feel defiant, praised, encouraged, crushed, supported, honored, abused, dismissed?

Some words spoken to us or about us have a huge effect. You may have carried such words with you for years, embedded inside you and resounding quietly within, undermining self-confidence and your ability to be your true sexual self. There are probably several phrases you can recall word for word, each time reliving or recalling the wound those words created.

Choose one thing that was said about your sexuality which still hurts when you recall it. It may have been a general statement about women, or personally directed to you. It could have been said to you, or something you overheard or came to hear later, reported back to you. It may have been recently, or tens of years ago. Try to choose the words that are the least healed, the most hurtful of all those words you have been recalling.

The following ritual has three sentences, spoken aloud one by one. Part of the power in this ritual lies in the sentences not being diluted with other talking; with justification, explanation or any kind of moderating of their effect. If you are doing this ritual with someone else, make it clear before you begin that you will only be speaking the three sentences and they will have to complete their actions without assistance from you.

These three sentences are the magical actions of the Third Cord, so bring all of your intent and focus into them.

Thinking of the most hurtful thing said to you or about you, regarding your sexuality, begin the process. Speak aloud, starting the sentence with "They said –". For example, you might say: *They said women were too sexual* or *They said I was fat* or *They said I should be grateful for any attention.*

As you speak, feel the resonances in your body of those words.

Now take up the Third Cord – or if you are doing this process with someone else have them take up the cord – and bind it around your body, in the place you feel hurts the most, hearing those words. If someone else is doing this for you, they should choose where to bind you according to their observation, without discussing it with you. Feel how it is to be restricted by those words that were spoken.

There were consequences to those words. Some of those consequences may still be playing out in your life; in your attitudes to yourself and your sexuality. Certainly there were consequences at the time; feelings and thoughts formed, decisions and judgments made.

The second sentence is about those consequences and it begins "And I felt –". For example, your second sentence might be: *And I felt ashamed to be a woman* or *And I felt humiliated that I could never be beautiful* or *And I felt angry and I wanted to pay them back.* Speak your second sentence aloud, giving your feelings all the weight they deserve.

When you have spoken the second sentence aloud, bind the cord that's around your body tightly, and knot it in place. If someone is with you, have them do this for you when you finish your second sentence. Feel how it is to be bound into those words and your feelings.

But you know now – and perhaps you even knew at the time – that what they said was not true. You are the one who knows the truth underneath what was said. The third sentence begins "But the truth is –". For example, your third sentence might be: *But the truth is my sexuality is wild and free and they were afraid* or

But the truth is I was beautiful then and am beautiful now or *But the truth is I give and receive pleasure only when I choose.*

When you have spoken (or even shouted) the truth and felt its resonance all through your body – and most particularly in that part of your body where you are bound by the cord – undo the knot and release yourself. Feel how freeing it is to take off that binding and breathe deeply. Even if someone is with you, it's important to undo the cord yourself.

Now, still holding the Third Cord, think of those words of truth you just spoke.

Name the cord with a single word that truly describes your sexuality. It may be a word you have just spoken in this ritual or it may be another word that comes to you. If you cannot think of a word, use the word *truth*.

Record the ritual in your Journal, especially the three sentences you spoke and the name of your Third Cord. Place the cord with the other two and then complete your ritual (giving thanks, closing the circle, grounding the energy and blowing out any candles). If you have shared this ritual with someone, thank and acknowledge them for bearing witness to your work.

I found this exercise particularly difficult as my emotions were very close to the surface and I have many issues from abuse. However, I have made some decisions to approach my sexuality differently and honestly.
    Shelley

It is possible this ritual will bring to the surface memories that have been long suppressed or never acknowledged, even by yourself. These may be memories of abuse, rape or incest. Speaking the truth is the first step towards healing but to support that truth you will probably need to take further steps. You can find a wise friend to talk to; phone a Rape Crisis Centre or Lifeline number (listed in your telephone directory) or make an appointment with a counselor for further guidance. If this happens to you it is because you are now ready and able to deal with this part of your truth. It's important you take the necessary steps to support yourself in integrating this truth and healing its trauma.

Speaking Out with the Voice of Truth

These activities can be done after you have completed your Third Cord or at any time during the remainder of your work with this book.

Your Sexual Truth

You can do this exercise in writing first if you like but it is really important at some stage to speak aloud. Consider if you might ask a trusted friend or your partner to listen (in either of these cases you can do it as an exchange, so each of you has a turn speaking and listening) or if you really can't find another person, at the very least speak it aloud looking into the mirror.

Give yourself ten minutes to speak the truth about your sexuality. You might choose to tackle a topic that has been on your mind, you might choose to speak of your sexual history or you might transport yourself forward in time and speak of the sexuality you hope to cultivate in yourself and how you imagine that will be.

Try to speak for the whole ten minutes. If you are silent for part of it, imagine what words, experiences and truths are not being spoken in your silence and ask yourself why you choose that. Reach more deeply into yourself for some true statements about your sexuality, even if they are not joined up into any story. See if you can express truths that usually stay hidden, cloaked in respectability, conventionality or shyness. Remember, what you are speaking is simply the truth about your own body and sexual self. If you are ashamed or embarrassed, that is a good starting point; try to express where the shame or embarrassment comes from and why you are carrying it. Then go deeper, into what rests underneath those cover-up emotions.

It's crucial the listeners don't speak at all, even to encourage or affirm you. It's important to have the experience of speaking the truth of your sexuality, rather than interacting with others. Afterwards you may be inspired to discuss sexual issues with friends or a partner, but at this moment you are completing the work of your Third Cord, voicing your truth about your sexuality.

I have and still am healing in so many ways... I was date raped for my first sexual intercourse experience and before that I was taken aside by one of the older boys in my school and was forced to touch him till he ejaculated. How does one move on to a healthy, fulfilling sexual relationship in one's life without one's SISTEARS who sit with you in safe sacred space and allow one to process the hurt, the guilt and all the other emotions one has locked into the cellular memory...
Tanna

Speak Truth

Think of people you owe truth to. Your children, partner or close friends are good places to start. Do you tell them how you truly feel about them? Do you share with them some of your own fears and doubts, your humanness, your vulnerabilities?

Make a resolution to speak nothing but the truth for a certain amount of time. My son did this for one day – it's one thing to say you will speak ONLY the truth, but to say you will SPEAK the truth (even when normally you would keep silent)... He found that aspect more challenging than sticking to the truth.

Examine the role of truth in your life. Do you expect it from others? Your children, partner or boss? What kind of truth do you expect, and what kind do you give? The whole-truth-and-nothing-but-the-truth kind of truth, or a truth that doesn't involve direct lying? Is this the kind of truth you prefer receiving?

How would your life be different if you spoke only the truth and the whole truth?

*For a long time now I have been involved in writing, public infor-
mation and storytelling about gay subjects for both gay and non-gay
audiences. Strange though it sounds, this does not make it that much
easier to tell the facts about my own sexuality... I know how ignored I
feel watching all those images of heterosexual romance... But the
lesbian scene is not that comforting either... Spirituality is a dirty
secret and women's issues easily dismissed as 'straight' or 'weak'.*
Berin

Resources

- *Aphrodite's Daughters: Women's Sexual Stories and the
  Journey of the Soul,* Jalaja Bonheim. Fireside, 1997
- *Listen to Me, Listen to You,* Anne Kotzman and Mandy
  Kotzman. Penguin Global, 2008
- *Loving What Is: Four Questions That Can Change Your Life,*
  Byron Katie. Three Rivers Press, 2003
- *The Courage to Heal: A Guide for Women Survivors of Child
  Sexual Abuse.* Ellen Bass and Laura Davis. Collins Living,
  2008
- Toastmasters International www.toastmasters.org

FOURTH STRAND: IN THE HEART

I think this part of the work was the most powerful... to actually state an intention of coming from the heart – took courage – and in a way it took none at all.

Catriona

Love love love. Love makes the world go round; love the one you're with; love is all there is; love is in the air... Love is everywhere. And love's a good thing, we all agree on that. People's love for their children, for dolphins and forests and fresh air and water may be enough to save the planet, never mind make life worth living and every day worth getting up for.

We think about love a lot. But how much do we do it? How many of our activities and thoughts are not just motivated by love but filled with love, done with love and within the spirit of enhancing love?

Love isn't always sweetness and light. We don't have to waft around in a haze, praising everything and never being angry, gutsy or raw to be loving. Love can be strong, bold, outraged; can be tender or torn, as well as warm and caring. Love can mean you shout at your child, because it's the only way to get the message through. Love can mean you become an impoverished artist rather than a wealthy business woman; love can mean you stay by someone's side through a drawn-out or even agonized dying, loving to be there.

Discovering the Heart of Love

I had often wondered about the nature of unconditional love. How is it that we are able to love our children this way and yet it's so difficult to apply in adult relationships? What would it be like to love someone for their core being, and know I would get no return for it? How could I unpick *relationship* from real love?

I learnt more about this when a very dear friend removed himself from our friendship. We had been close in an easy, delighted way where we shared an excitement about each other's ideas and understandings of the world and it didn't matter how long the gaps were between our conversations. I had treasured those conversations, his caring of me and his unique qualities.

When he stopped relating to me I was deeply hurt. In the absence of our conversations I became varyingly angry, distressed, indifferent and judgmental. I remembered all the other men who had cut off from me, abandoned me. I remembered how important being true was to him, and I felt he had compromised that truthfulness. When faced with him, however – even across the street or in a crowded room – I found what I had been feeling melted away as if it never existed, to be replaced purely by the pleasure I had always felt upon seeing him.

What was this pleasure? It was no longer the anticipation of a good conversation; we spoke only briefly and awkwardly. It was not the pleasure of remembrance, nostalgia for the closeness we had shared; each time I was brought sharply into the present, where that closeness, if it still existed, could not be expressed. It was not a pleasure connected with how he felt for me for I no longer had any idea what he felt or what I meant to him. It seemed to be – it had to be – purely a pleasure in his existence. He existed, and when I was confronted with his existence I was happy.

In between instances of seeing him I would sometimes decide to challenge him on this stranded friendship, or express my hurt or demand reassurance. Each time I saw him whatever words I had determined on lost all interest for me; they could not touch how it actually was. Seeing him I was made happy. And in happiness my need disappeared, even my need for our friendship and our connection.

After five years or so his circumstances changed and an

awkward, occasional communication occurred when our paths crossed. These conversations – unplanned, uncertain as to existence, length or any future – still contained the flavor of my happiness. I clearly remember thinking that perhaps, if I added all our future conversations together for the rest of my life, they might add up to a length of a few hours. And that did not occur to me as meager or negligible; I felt joy and anticipation at the richness and pleasure of those few hours, sprinkled randomly through years.

This is the man who became my partner. When we finally began a relationship I was amazed to discover I felt no trepidation at all; because I knew the most important thing was my love, and not any response he might have to it. I felt unshakable in our relating because my love was so simple, based on his mere existence and independent from his relationship to me.

Of course things are more complex now. I can no longer make such grand statements. Now I feel many layers of love, knowledge and need in relation to him and some of these are conditional. His behavior can easily affect my feelings towards him. But underneath I know and almost always feel the original threads of that pure love, wrought in absence and difficulty, where I discovered I did not love him for what he was to me or how he was towards me, but for who he was.

My assessment of this contains an awareness of his own heart, for I believe one of the reasons I was incapable of feeling anything but pleasure in his existence was because of something fundamental within him. He believes that experiencing love is the deepest part of human life and I have to imagine all those times we didn't speak or barely interacted, that was what he was doing. His knowledge of love somehow enabled me to find my own – and it was not to do with actions or thoughts but only a lived experience of joy.

Love Examined

What is the true nature of love? Is it selfless? Do we love another person regardless of their involvement with us, even if they are fulfilling none of our needs? Or is love more pragmatic, the everyday business of caring for and interacting with another? One person thinks love is a series of actions (you love someone, therefore you look after them); another person knows it as a feeling; someone else understands it as the vibrational essence that everything can be reduced to; some think of it as another word for God (or Goddess) and others see love as the life-force itself. Perhaps these interpretations are not even contradictory but just different ways of viewing the same thing.

My partner is disbelieving that I can be affected by what seem to him completely mundane things, such as his mending my shoes, or cleaning my car. But I am bowled over by his love for me, as expressed in such actions and every time I wear those shoes or get in my car, I experience it as an almost tangible thing.

This is where it gets complex, because he probably doesn't even notice most of the acts of service I perform for him, and certainly he wouldn't count them as any expression of love. It's as if my love – or anyone's love – has to be translated into a language the other person can understand. Unless you are able to take the broadest sweep and say it's all love and you feel the intentions, so it doesn't matter how it's expressed.

To experience love in your life it has often been suggested it is your own loving that counts, rather than anyone else's love for you. Your love for the world and life; your love for others; love for yourself; spiritual love. It seems when we are expressing and feeling love is when we most deeply receive its benefits – not when others are feeling it for us, or expressing it to us. Think how full your heart feels when you go into the bedroom of a sleeping child, when you summon up the faces of those you love best, when you find exactly the right gift for someone or when you are able to make a difference to someone else's life.

Once we say that it is *our* love and loving (rather than other people's) that are the important signifiers, our potential experience of love becomes unlimited. If we measure our happiness or fulfillment through whether other people love us – or the right people love us, or love us in the right way, or express it in the right way – we are always tentative, always tied to that and in any moment it can be withdrawn, or change, or become unavailable. When we say this measure of happiness or fulfillment rests solely within ourselves, no such anxieties remain. Now we are focused on feeling the fullness of our own love and expressing it however we choose: Through dance; art; words and acts of love, tenderness and passion; doing good works or opening our heart into an energetic flow with the universe.

I am aware the perpetrators of various crimes – including murder, incest and abuse – frequently claim to have loved the victims of their crimes. This type of crime against another comes from a place of need and power, of putting the desires of oneself above the rights of another. It is not love. To offer love in this situation is not an adequate response.

We have to divorce abuse from our understanding of what love is. One way to extricate these masquerades of love is to ask the question: *Is loving this other person compatible with loving myself?* If loving the other person means to act unlovingly to yourself (placing yourself in physical danger, emotional neglect or psychological trauma) then this type of *love* is not what we are searching for when we talk about unconditional love. The type of love that is threatened by your own healthy self-love is a desperate, needy love, seeking a fulfillment that will not and cannot be met. The very place that healthy and respectful love comes from – a sense of confidence in yourself and awareness of your loving and essential loveableness – is threatened or even destroyed in abusive relationships.

Let us think of love as being part of the force that animates our universe, part of the tide of life that gave birth to us and the best part of ourselves, that we offer as a gift wherever and whenever we can. It can be demarcated by being observed to be freely given and freely taken. Love is the offering life makes back to life.

Approaching the Heart of Love

These activities are the lead-in to the Fourth Cord. Do as many of them as you can.

Look at what you already love; the people, places and activities you love. By directing your attention towards these things and actively developing your relationship to them, you open your heart further and explore some of its depths. Sometimes you will even experience an expansion, or flow-on of love, into areas you didn't set out to affect.

Loving People, Places and Activities

People You Love

Write a list of people you love in your Journal. Looking at the list, decide on three or four of these people who – even though you love them – don't receive as much attention from you as you would really like to give, or feel they deserve.

Write the name of each person you have chosen in the middle of a blank page. Now all around it (use colored pens or pencils if you'd like) write all the things that you love, admire and respect about them. Decorate your page with motifs or a border that reminds you of that person.

Then create a gift for each person: Take them out to lunch; make them a card; mow their lawn; give them a massage. Make it clear you are giving this because of how you feel about them.

Places You Love

In your Journal write a list of places you love, focusing especially on nearby places you rarely take the time to enjoy, or places that are just a little out of your way so you seldom go there. It might even be your own backyard!

Choose two of these places that are accessible to you. Devote a page to each one in your Journal, maybe drawing the place – this can be an energetic impression rather than a literal drawing – or pasting a photo in. Write down what it is you love.

Then decide on a way to express your love for each place. If it is publicly owned you might choose to do a clean-up there, gathering and removing rubbish. If it is your own backyard you could begin a vegetable or herb garden you have yearned for, or paint a mural on the fence.

If your chosen place is somewhere like a beach or a forest you can create an Altar, made only from the resources around you. The beach is a great place for an Altar to Aphrodite – you can draw or build the Altar in sand, adding arrangements of shells, seaweed... whatever you find. In the forest you can make an Altar at the base of a tree or in a small grove, arranging leaves, seedpods and other things into a mandala-type pattern or a circle with the directions marked out and special offerings in the centre for the Goddess and the local spirits of the place.

If a place you love is under threat or desperately needs some public money or attention you might choose to write a letter to the paper, or to your local member of parliament or other relevant authority about it. You could participate in an activity at your chosen place – maybe Tai Chi, a playgroup, surfing lesson or tree planting session.

You might choose simply to go there and spend an afternoon meditating, or visit daily for a week. Once I walked a local labyrinth every day for a week; each day I took a photo and recorded the chant I used as I walked it and put these together in my Journal. My relationship to the labyrinth is now much richer because of that week when I got to be there in rain, early in the morning, with other people and by myself. Just the action of turning up day after day deepened my appreciation for it as well as my knowledge of it.

Activities You Love

On a new page in your Journal write a list of activities you love the most. Try for at least a dozen. Once you've written the list go through it again and put a star next to every activity you wish you did more often.

Choose three activities with stars next to them – try to make it a broad range; one might be a physical activity, one mental or creative and one a social activity. Put circles around these items.

Devote a new page in your Journal to each of these activities. Write down how the activity makes you feel, how you came to love it and why you don't do enough of it.

Now look at these activities, one by one. How can you arrange to include each one (more) in your life? Sometimes it's a matter of rearranging priorities or timetables but it can be more difficult. What if you've written 'overseas travel' but haven't any money? Draw up a timeline and a savings plan; even if you are planning for a trip in three years it is now included within the things you are doing and will add its flavor to your life.

What if you've written 'making love' but you haven't a partner? Take it seriously, is the first thing. Ask yourself some more questions; what is it you love or miss so much about love-making? Is it the touch? Intimacy? The sensuality? Depending on your answer, find a way to construct experiences for yourself that give you some of these things – visiting a spa, receiving a massage or beauty treatment, maybe a weekend away with your best friend. Make love to yourself in the way you hope someday a partner will make love to you – have candles in the bedroom, sleep in beautiful sheets, rub delicious oils into your body. And for some people a workout at the gym is more fulfilling than scented baths!

Sometimes what you write will force you to re-evaluate your life deeply. Perhaps you've written that you'd love to have a dog, take long walks in the bush and have a flower garden, but you live in a high-rise in the middle of the city? Take time to seriously reconsider your life. If you decide you must remain where you are, dedicate yourself to getting into the country on weekends, to looking after friends' dogs when they go away and to window boxes.

Make a space for these activities in your life. Do more of the things you love. Spend time with people you love and in places you love. All these things make it easier to open your heart; to feel, offer and receive love from all directions – from the wind and sun, from your friends and family, from yourself, the world and the divine. If you have children you can include them in many of these activities; you are teaching them how important it is to do lovely, fulfilling things, not just duties and necessities.

The Love/Fear Dance

Time: 30 minutes to an hour

You will need: Courage (Journal and pen optional)

I vividly remember the first time someone said to me that all actions – every single one – can be divided into coming from love or coming from fear. I thought it indescribably naive and yet the idea grabbed hold of me and has never quite let go. I still think it is not sufficiently complex – but if something is as useful as this is, does it matter if it is expressed simplistically? At its heart, it works.

Take any action of your own: Feeding the cats in the morning; making your child's sandwiches; writing your emails; driving to work; paying at the supermarket checkout. Now ask yourself: *How would that action be different if I did it with love?* For example each time I make my son's school lunch I'm a bit distracted and somewhat hurried. If I ask the question, how would it be different done with love, a feeling of pleasure comes into my arms and I find myself smiling as I look for the dried apricots, not irritatedly pushing jars aside. I'm sure it must make some difference to the lunch, but most importantly it makes a difference to me, to how I feel about making the lunch and how I feel afterwards.

Next, take an action of yours during which you feel reluctant, tight or unwilling. Phoning someone you really don't want to talk to; asking a favor; reprimanding a child or finally organizing the files on your computer. How would these things be different if you came from a place of love? I wouldn't phone that person until I had found a place of universal love within me, from which I could send at least a thread out to them… and then I'm sure the conversation would be easier, at least for me but probably both of us.

But what about when real fear is a tangible part of the equation? What if I'm afraid of being in the house on my own, or traveling in Asia or confronting my lover with an aspect of his behavior I don't like? What if I'm afraid of rejection, pain or loss? Then the difference between the two scenarios – operating from fear and operating from love – begins to widen dramatically.

If I am in fear in the house on my own, I am anxious and my shoulders are tight. I feel paranoid and irrational and can't placate that fear. If I come from a place of love I automatically begin to look after myself. I take sensible precautions; locking the doors, keeping a phone near my bed or a light on. Maybe I install better locks or an alarm and get to know the neighbors. I tap into a larger sense of being cared for, of being held in universal love, light and energy and I consciously breathe it in and surround myself with it, fill the house with it. Then I more or less stop worrying.

Take a real fear of yours and ask yourself the question: *How would my actions around this fear be different if I came from a place of love?* Pay attention to your answers. Record them in your Journal, if you like.

Confronting other people is a common and everyday fear. Fear can obscure our behavior, as we try to control the outcome. When we come from a place of love, our attitude conveys that we're not too stressed about it. Then maybe the other person is less inclined to be defensive. Even when we are afraid of rejection, pain and loss, to come from a place of love creates a safe landing place, an internal reassurance that is supportive and strengthening.

It seems obvious – but mostly overlooked – to say the more actively you feel love, the less room there is for fear and therefore the less governed you are by fear. When your actions are not flavored with fear, the results of those actions will stem less from a reaction to fear. By deliberately choosing love in your actions, you choose all the consequences of those actions to be influenced by (your own) love and you invite the ripple effect – that the love will spread outwards.

Preparation for the Heart of Love

Time: Allow an hour, which includes time for dancing
For the Fourth Cord you will need:

- A mirror (not a hand mirror) or another person to work with
- Music you feel is heart-opening that plays for at least 20 minutes (it can be over several tracks). Not love songs – especially not anguished ones – but perhaps achingly beautiful solo flutes, the sound of waves crashing onto the shore or recordings of whales singing to each other. You may choose chanting, even in another language; it's your heart that has to respond to it, not your mind.
- Choose a colored cord for your heart. It might be a soft pink; green, which is the traditional color for the heart chakra or any other color which symbolizes the heart to you. Measure it out to the length of your other cords, cut it and knot the ends.
- Your Aphrodite Altar
- Your Journal and pen
- Read through the whole process before starting. If you are

working with another person, make sure they have also read through the whole process.

I remember getting the idea that opening my heart needs courage, but that I was strong enough to choose to take that risk. It has certainly had a huge impact on my life as I started a new relationship not long after… and I spent the first few months in the terror of letting myself be touched as I was, and had to make lots of conscious efforts to open my heart, and try to trust that whatever was coming, I would be able to deal with.
    Diane

The Fourth Cord: Love
(*With thanks to David Deida, for inspiration*)
This is the central work of this chapter.

Cast your circle, light the candles on your Altar and say a prayer to Aphrodite, or else do whatever preparation and energy raising you prefer.

Spend a few moments revising the first three cords in your mind, especially if it has been days or weeks since you did them. Say their names over in your mind and wear them looped about your waist, hips or around your neck.

Start the music and lie down comfortably with your Fourth Cord. Put a cushion under your head and a blanket over you, if you need. Hold the cord over your heart with your hands quite close together so just a short piece of cord, about a hand span's width, is stretched between your hands, with the rest of the cord falling away to either side.

Allow the music to simply wash over you at the beginning. Be aware of the circle you have cast around yourself, your Altar and your connection to the ground and the earth. Breathe into your body and feel it relax.

After a few minutes of breathing bring your awareness to the area of your heart, where your hands and your cord lie. Perhaps you can feel or sense your heartbeat. Imagine your heart within your body and think of it as a fountain or well of unlimited, recycling love; imagine that just as your heart pumps blood around your body, so does it channel love, both for yourself and beyond yourself.

Listening to the music, allow your heart to relax and open. Over the next ten minutes try expanding this feeling of heart-opening so it ripples through your body – all through your chest and upper body, then out through your arms, up through your head and down through your stomach, hips and genitals and down your legs.

Let the music flow through you and through your heart, until you can feel it in your fingertips and toes and then imagine this heart energy continuing to flow, so it gently pulses beyond your body, like a breathing aura expanding out from your whole being. You might imagine this as a rainbow or in heart colors or the color of your cord; and you might feel it in waves, ripples or other sensations, such as that of warmth. Feel yourself stretch into it.

For the last five minutes of the music just lie there encompassed by your heart energy, allowing it to relax, refresh and recharge your whole being.

When the music has finished sit up, either facing your mirror or the other person. This person may be purely supporting you, or also doing the process (take turns, if this is the case). Hold the Fourth Cord over your heart again, with about a hand span of cord held tautly between your hands and the rest of the cord falling away to either side.

The following process correlates the idea of an open heart with the length of the cord displayed between your two hands. If your hands are very close together, with only a short piece of cord between them, that will signify your heart is mostly closed. The wider apart you move your hands (and thus the more of the

Fourth Cord is stretched between them) the more it will signify an open heart. You may find your hands moving together as often as they move apart, even very quickly after they have opened out. When this happens breathe into your heart again and feel the opening, that *stretch* you found previously.

Whatever your truth is in that moment, demonstrate it with your hands on the cord. If you are doing this process by yourself you will see this reflected in the mirror. If you are doing it with someone else it will signal to them how open or closed your heart is in any one moment and will assist them in their role of offering openings to you.

Opening your heart is the magical step for the Fourth Cord, so bring all of your intent and focus to it.

Name an issue in your personal life that you feel stuck in. This should be an unresolved issue you are not sure how to progress with. It may be long-standing: *I don't know how to talk to my mother* or recent: *I'm worried the lines on my face make me look old.* It can be very personal: *I don't know how to ask for what I like in sex* or seemingly mundane: *I'm bored with my work.*

Now holding that issue clearly in your mind, demonstrate with your hands on the cord how open your heart is in the situation you have named. Probably your hands stay quite close together, perhaps they even get closer than they were to start with.

Working Alone
If you are doing the process by yourself (looking into a mirror), choose a quality you feel you rarely display in this situation – it might be *courage, humor, vision, power, softness, hurt* – and name it aloud to yourself. Don't think very deeply; it's better to name the first one that comes to you to keep the process moving. You will have lots of opportunity to name other qualities as you continue.

Working With Someone Else

If you are doing the process with another person they name the qualities. They do this by saying: "I would like to see more of your..." and naming a quality. Breathe into each quality that is offered to you without judging it and feel what difference, if any, it makes to your heart-opening. They should continue naming qualities without too long a pause between each one.

For example, imagine the quality *courage* has been spoken. Think of *courage* as a tangible thing you can access within yourself and breathe into your heart. Holding the original situation clearly in your mind, try deliberately breathing in *courage* – and feel what difference that makes to the openness of your heart. Show any changes with your hands on the cord.

After several deep breaths and when you have felt the impact of that particular quality, move fairly quickly to the next quality. Simply name aloud another quality – it might be purely intuitive or it may be something you know you do not bring to the situation – it could be *patience* or *self-love* or *wisdom*. Then again breathe that quality into your heart and demonstrate on the cord how open your heart becomes.

Keep breathing and naming qualities to enable you to stretch out your heart energy. The qualities you name may even seem exact opposites – you may name *patience* and then *anger* – that doesn't matter in the quest to find and remove the blockages you have had on opening your heart. Work with this process for five minutes or so and aim to get your hands as wide apart as you can, still thinking of the issue you have chosen and breathing in qualities.

When the time is up, or when your arms are stretched wide apart and you do not feel the need to keep bringing them closer together protectively, defensively or reactively, take a snapshot of your current feeling. Look at yourself in the mirror, if you are using one. Remind yourself of the issue you have chosen and how you feel now in relation to that issue.

Put the cord down and record in your Journal the issue, your feelings at the beginning and end of this process and any insights you have had.

One option is to repeat this exercise with a second issue. If you found the first time either very difficult or very easy, this is advisable; also if you would like to get some more practice at opening your heart. Try a quite different issue; a work issue if you started with a personal issue, or a practical issue if you began with a spiritual or emotional one. Again record your beginning and finishing positions and any insights in your Journal.

When you have completed this process sit holding your Fourth Cord. Name the cord with a word that represents the newest or most startling thing that has come to you through the process. Thus its name may be one of the qualities you called in or any other word that sums up the difference you felt in yourself after the opening. If no other word comes to you, you can choose the name *heart* or *open*.

It was like fresh air and renewal.
  Artemesia

Listen to your heart-opening music a second time – or continue with the music, if you stopped it part-way before – and this time dance a dedication to the opening of your heart. Dance with your cords around your waist, hips or neck; or leave them lying on the Altar if you prefer.

When you finish make sure to ground your energy, blow out any candles and close your circle.

Opening Further into Love
This is an optional activity. It's good to do after you have completed your Fourth Cord and you can continue to practice it throughout the

remainder of your work with this book (or even the remainder of your life).

Heart-Opening in Real Life

The continuing work of the heart is to consciously practice, in at least three different situations, an application of the process you learnt. Try it in a difficult moment, or a situation you feel limited by, stuck in or uncertain as to how to proceed. This may be a relationship dynamic (make sure at least one of them is – it can be with your child, lover, relative or work colleague), a spiritual or personal matter or something more general. Keep your breathing deep and steady and name to yourself some qualities to embody whilst trying all the time to open your heart.

It's preferable to do this before moving onto the next chapter. Record your experiences in your Journal.

It's also worth asking your heart what it needs to be more open. Perhaps it will want you to spend more time on reflection and healing; to take up an exercise program; pursue your creativity or show your love more openly. See how you can support your heart, by working to help its – and your – opening.

The process of opening my heart has influenced my life in very profound ways. I realized that I tend to close my heart when I'm grieving, when I'm afraid, when I feel insecure. But when I manage to open my heart in this way, grief does not get stuck but flows in and out of me. Fear doesn't lead to a panic attack, but flows and departs like a wave. And insecurity does not make me automatically defend myself, but is a feeling that comes and goes. Opening my heart is opening to life's flow. When I take the time for myself and sit in stillness, I manage to do this more and more.
  Miriam

Resources

- *Dear Lover: A Woman's Guide to Men, Sex and Love's Deepest Bliss*, David Deida. Sounds True, 2006
- *Love After Love: Stages of Loving*, Paula P. Hardin. New World Library, 1996
- *Passionate Marriage: Keeping Love and Intimacy Alive in Committed Relationships*, David Schnarch. Holt Paperbacks, 1998
- *Rumi: The Book of Love: Poems of Ecstasy and Longing*, Coleman Barks, John Moyne, Nevit Ergin, Reynold Nicholson and M. G. Gupta. HarperOne, 2005
- *The Conscious Heart: Seven Soul-Choices that Inspire Creative Partnership*, Kathlyn Hendricks & Gay Hendricks. Bantam, 1999
- *Women Who Love Too Much*, Robin Norwood. Pocket, 2008

FIFTH STRAND: DANCING THE BODY

The more I dance, the more in tune with my body I am.
  Artemesia

We often behave as if the body is secondary to mind or spirit. But the body houses the mind; the body houses spirit. We have no particular evidence that either mind or spirit can exist *without* body. Spirit and mind may well be parts of the body; or the body an aspect of them. Either way, the body deserves no less attention, no less honor, respect and reverence than the mind and spirit.

I believe it is our dualistic thinking that leads us to imagine these things are separate, rather than aspects of the whole. We can think of a tree as separate from the forest, or humans as separate from the earth. But we can also see the tree is part of the forest and humans are part of the earth. So it may be that these distinctions of *body, spirit* and *mind* might be a matter of perspective. If we allow them to be simply parts of our whole self, they have an opportunity to work in harmony.

It can be quite difficult to distinguish *body* from beauty and appearance. But this is about body, *body*, BODY – how it is to be in the body, within it and of it; to be this body. Not how it looks. This body that has breasts and hips, a womb, vagina and clitoris... as well as hands that are so wonderful; feet and legs that carry us around; an amazing back holding the whole thing together; a head with its many attributes; all that skin and bone and beating blood; those veins and tendons and muscles...

My Dance with Body

I've taken a long time to come to terms with my body. I don't mean how it looks, but being in it at all. As a teenager I had juvenile arthritis and experienced varying degrees of pain in my body but mainly, overwhelmingly, in my feet. From the age of about twelve until I was nineteen, I could rarely walk without some level of discomfort. Walking back from school I would often be crying with pain before I reached home. There were times when I was so overwhelmed by the meaningless nature of chronic pain I wept helplessly for hours at a time.

At school I was excused from sport and suffered through the plays I loved. Standing on stage was sometimes excruciating, especially those winter performances, but I was prepared to sacrifice my feet for the theatre. At rehearsals I sat down every instant I didn't have to be standing; sometimes I could barely get off the stage before falling over from pain. In moments when the play came to life I forgot all that and experienced transcendence. I think it paved the way for my later involvement in ritual.

I didn't find an answer to my arthritis for many years. I discovered that heat helped, massage helped, dry and warm weather helped. I eliminated the pain completely with a virulent drug which I agreed to take for three months (later I found out this drug is usually only prescribed to much older people because of its cumulative side effects). Then at nineteen I went to a naturopath and discovered changing my diet could eliminate the pain.

I was an instant convert. About five days into my no dairy; no tomatoes or potatoes, eggplant or capsicum; no coffee or alcohol, sugar, spices or salt; no chicken or red meat; no wheat; no mushrooms; no citrus diet I felt the pain ebb away and I never looked back. It was a remarkably easy diet to keep. One slip and the twinges would return as a warning. After a few years my body could tolerate some of those things again, in small doses; some – tomatoes, wheat and potatoes – I continued avoiding for the next ten years.

My eyes changed color. Originally I had hazel eyes – brownish with dashes of green – and they changed, overnight it seemed to me. One day I saw in the mirror I had blue-grey eyes.

It was a few months after I'd begun the diet and it looked as if I had become a new person, from the inside out.

At around twenty-one I suffered repetitive strain injury (RSI) from typing and spent a few years barely able to write, for the pain shooting uncontrollably along my arms. My hands had always been my most precious body part, because of the writing, and all through my arthritic childhood I had bargained with fate; I was prepared to lose everything except the use of my hands. The RSI seemed to ridicule all that previous suffering.

I came down with glandular fever and spent three months in a haze of nothingness, then two years slowly recovering my normal strength. Gradually, gradually I won back bits of my own body, through physiotherapy, postural change and eventually a determination that I would come into the heritage of this body; I would claim it and love it and work with it to finally enjoy being in my body, on this planet, part of the earth.

So far as I've aged, my body has come into better and better condition and I've developed a closer relationship with it. I'm fitter now than I've ever been. I'm not at the mercy of chronic pain, though I regard it with great respect; I know it has the power to rewrite my mind, my understanding of myself and the world any time it strikes. Pain retains the power to shock me into awareness; there's this inescapable thing with my body; I can't get out of it. So I believe I'd better assimilate problems quickly or it leads to not wanting to be in the body; an untenable position for an earth-worshiping pagan.

About six years ago I twisted my right ankle very badly. It didn't – quite – break but the tiny ligaments were torn and damaged. I was on crutches for weeks and ever since then, that ankle has been fragile. Influenced by princess stories I read at a young age, I had never much liked my ankles. I was convinced girls' ankles should be slender and mine patently weren't. I had peasant ankles (along with my knees and thighs, although miraculously, not my wrists and fingers, which I always liked much better).

Three months or so after I'd damaged the ankle I thought it was about time it healed properly. I went to an acupuncturist. As he was examining my ankle I asked, casually, how long it would be before that awful swelling went away and my ankle resumed its normal shape.

"Oh, that's the shape it is, now," he said cheerfully and went on to explain about the tissue that builds up around injuries like this and how – once the initial swelling and bruising is gone – that's more or less it, for shape.

I was so horrified, lying there on the treatment table, I just blanked out my feelings. My left ankle (that I'd never liked because it was thick and clumpy) was now, by comparison, slender and shapely. Suddenly I loved it. I wondered why I hadn't loved it always and, even worse, why I hadn't appreciated the now eternally-damaged one all those years. I made a decision, still lying there in shock, that I loved my new ankle. Regardless and no regrets and no holding back. Oh – ankles – so functional, so practically beautiful, holding me up every step I take, damaged but reformed; oh I think they are beautiful, now.

My ankles are one of the few parts of myself I'd never admired. More usually I think I am an embodiment of the Goddess. Not because I am anything special, but because my understanding is that women are the Goddess, manifest on earth. But she tripped me up, literally, in a kind of coyote moment. Don't appreciate these wonderful ankles? – bam! Less wonderful ankles. Appreciate them yet? I've always respected the Dark Goddess and here she was, speaking directly through my body.

I think I learnt my lesson. I'm offering it to you in case there is a similar lesson awaiting you, perhaps about your hips, skin or teeth – could be anything. Love it all, because surely we realize by now that gravity and time do not improve the body. Luckily there's compensating factors in wisdom, understanding and a working knowledge, even appreciation of this body we were born into.

I feel more embodied… It is as though the Goddess came home to stay, to gently awaken me to her tenderness, to her supreme power, to her wisdom and ineffable beauty. There is something of silence and laughter in her presence with me.

  Kate

The Body Story

Skin has always been one of my favorite things – my own skin, my child's skin, the skin of my lover. I think it is amazing – the kind of wrapping of the whole thing – and can't quite ever believe the extent of its wonders. I love that it's so utterly functional and yet so sensual, so aesthetic. I love that it's tough and yet sensitive; so stretchy, pliant and adaptable but also holds such shape. Perhaps you admire bones, the grace of the skeleton; or muscles and the network of veins plumbing every part of the body; perhaps internal organs or the digestive system do it for you, or the wonders of the senses.

Monique Wittig's extraordinary book, *The Lesbian Body*, catalogues women's bodies in a way that transformed my understanding. In the world she creates, bones, inner organs and the layering of skin and blood vessels are the essence of female (human) beauty, as well as the inspiration of passion. She literally rewrites our cultural understanding of the female body.

We all experience times of physical grace and power; abseiling down a cliff, swimming in the river or doing yoga quietly in the morning. And most of us regard as special those times in love-making or dance where all mind, all questions and commentary depart and body is all there is, animal-like and elemental. Humans also have the universal experience of pain. This body leaves us vulnerable to accident, blood and physical hurt, little or agonizing; it is surely impossible to be human without pain.

Giving birth – when I could spare a thought – I was in raptures that nearly every woman born on the planet *no matter which country or how many thousands of years ago* had experienced this, this exact thing. I felt vast in that moment, eternal and patterned through time. Bodily extreme ripped away the differences in social conditioning, mental constructs and physical surrounds between me and all those other women; leaving just an essential, human (female) body experience.

I feel the same about being born – that *every single human being* has experienced this – and I expect to feel the same way about dying. Prior to birth, *every single human* has experienced nine months cradled within the body of a woman. This woman's body, entirely encompassing us, growing and nurturing us must be the earliest human experience and I think it is where a strong, essential knowledge of *goddess* comes from. We have been there – in the body of the Goddess.

At these levels, looks and appearance are utterly irrelevant. The color of skin is worth nothing, beside the miracle of skin. The size of breasts means nothing, compared with the function of breasts. The shape of the body is irrelevant when one considers the entirety of the human body.

Often we divide our experiences up – the body feels this, the mind thinks that – and one doesn't relate to the other. Or we feel something – love or sadness or ecstasy – but don't let our bodies express it. However much we believe we are truly spirit, however superior we may believe the mind to be, the reality is we are each in a body. A body that bleeds, weeps, breathes, lives and dies. A body that may – or may not – contain the intangibles of spirit, soul, mind but which inarguably is a body.

There are moments – for me they are dancing or making love or in ritual – but I have heard athletes talk of them, and artists; where the body is entire and perfect, where the contribution of every part of oneself – thought, muscles, heartbeat, perception – blends utterly together in actions that one experiences as the pinnacle of what is possible. There is no awareness of different parts, then. Rather one is utterly whole, not only within oneself but with the entire universe.

Is it enough to imagine a painting in the mind, or does one have to paint it? Is it enough to support a political action theoretically, or does one have to lend one's body to it? Is it enough to feel love, or is one almost compelled to express it, through hugs, tears, love-making, letter-writing, poetry or song? We are creatures of body. This earth-body we live on – that our own small bodies are composed of, with all their atoms, chemicals and microbes – we are born from this body and dying, return to it. Like trees in a forest, life animates us into individuality but we come from and return to the hummus of the earth, which will nurture the lives of others just as it nurtured ours.

Our bodies also come from our mothers' bodies, and theirs from their mothers'. I, writing this book and you, the women I am writing for, have a woman's body. At this level we are like the ancient Goddess figurines, most important for our bellies, hips and breasts. Whether or not you ever conceive, carry a child or give birth – you have that body. Our bodies are generative; fertile, sexual, nurturing. This is body, sacred body and sacred women's body; she who has come forth from the earth and who can make another's body, within her own. Women's bodies are the body of the Goddess.

I vividly remember feeling my strong, juicy body and seeing the other women shine with their own light and beauty.
   Miriam

Approaching the Body Dance
These activities are the lead-in to the Fifth Cord. It is recommended to do at least two of them.

My body is the body of the Goddess. This line is from a chant by Michael Stillwater. By the time you complete this cord it will become something you can sing, dance, feel and believe. Perhaps it will only come to you in short moments, visions or glimpses;

perhaps it will embrace your whole body and leave you in ecstasy before it fades; perhaps it will become a state of being you can choose to enter, in ritual or dance.

By now you have a long history with your body. Ask yourself how well you look after it, especially in its difficulties, or if you expect perfection from it and do your best to ignore or punish it when it falls short? Ask yourself how you would care for your child's body, if it had these same difficulties. Take this as a guide for caring for your own.

Appreciating the Body

Time: 30 minutes

You will need: Your Journal and pen

Begin a new page in your Journal headed *Body*.
Write three lists:

- A list of all the gifts your body has given you, from birth until this moment.
- A list of unhappiness or complaints you have had, with your body.
- A list of what your body currently requires from you.

After reading through these lists, try to sum up in a few sentences your relationship to your body. Write these sentences down. Now ask yourself: Is there anything you would like to change about how you treat your body? If so, make a note of this.

Down the bottom of the page, or on a new page, write a statement you imagine will apply *one year from now* that sums up your relationship to your body.

Underneath this you may wish to write some strategies or resolutions, or you may just like to finish with a *thank you* to your body.

Sacred Body Bathing

Time: Allow two hours
You will need: A bath and ingredients for the bath (details below)

Many books of rituals, spells and self-love suggest taking a special bath.

Don't follow any recipes except your own for this one – where, when and how would it be most special for *you* to have a sacred bath? How would you know it was sacred? Would it be the special candle you lit, the oils you used, what you did before and afterwards?

Here are some suggestions – but no recipes. Write your own recipe and record it in your Journal. Perhaps even scent the page with an oil you use, or stick in some of the same petals you have in your bath.

Suggestions for creating a unique sacred bath:
Before and After: This will depend on the time of day you have your bath. If it is a late night bath, you probably want to go to bed afterwards and wrap yourself into dreams. Beforehand, however, you could have done a whole evening of ritual – or not, as you choose.

Give some thought to whether you want your bath to *be* the ritual, or be *part* of a ritual – and if so, what you will be doing before and after the bath. This could include cooking yourself a special meal; spending time writing in your Journal or meditating; dancing by yourself or massaging parts of your body (legs, feet, hands, face and scalp are all easy to massage yourself); or doing things you usually don't have enough time for (rearranging the contents of your drawers, putting photos into albums or writing letters or e-mails to those you love).

If you want your bath to be only part of a ritual it can be the central part – the main event, so to speak – just book-ended by a ritual invocation to begin and followed by self-massage or writing in your Journal. Otherwise a bath can be used at the beginning of a ritual, as a cleansing and clearing of all old energies, thoughts and habits; or at the end of a ritual as a relaxation and a chance to let your intention and ritual work really soak into you.

Intention: Spend some time – perhaps even whilst you are running the bathwater – deciding on your intention for this ritual bath. It may be a simple intention such as pleasure, relaxation or nurture. Or perhaps it is more complex; to wash away past loves and relationships, or to rediscover your sensual self. You should record your intention in your Journal, along with your bath recipe and any thoughts, feelings or realizations that come to you during the bath.

The Bath: Is there an outside bath you can use? A pool, a grotto? Your own bath, or if you don't have one, a friend's bath you can borrow?

The Time: If it's your own bath it can be any time of day, but make it a special time; perhaps dusk, or midnight or early morning. If you have access to an outside bath, bathing by moonlight or starlight is magical. If you're using a friend's bath, make sure it is at a time when you won't feel rushed or as if you're inconveniencing anyone – perhaps when they are at work, or away for a weekend – pre-arranged, of course!

The Details

Candles - most people are keen on candles with baths – you could use a candle you have used in ritual before or one specially prepared for this occasion, even with a spell or invocation carved into it. Perhaps you prefer many tea lights scattered about the room or to bathe in complete darkness.

Oils – or bubble bath if you prefer – choose a ready-prepared bath oil or make your own, adding a few drops of one or two essential oils to a spoonful or more of base oil such as almond oil or apricot kernel oil. The base oil means you will emerge from the bath coated with a fine layer of oil, which you can then rub into your skin or towel off. Essential oils are much nicer than imitation scents (at the moment I like a mixture of rosemary and lavender, but rose oil is lovely, as are citrus oils). There are dozens to choose from in health food and similar shops.

Additions – rose petals are lovely, or you could use petals from other flowers, especially if they come from your own garden. I once had a bath with cinnamon sticks broken up and scattered into the bath. Vanilla has a strong and enticing scent. To be outrageous, add food coloring, glitter/sparkles or maybe a liter of milk! This is not even mentioning the possibilities of plastic ducks, bath pillows, back scrubbers...

Atmosphere – music or silence? Fresh hot towels waiting for you to emerge? Incense? Decorations – crystals, an Altar, something beautiful to gaze at?

Intention Again – you can choose your ingredients for fun (what about milk, rose petals, rose essence AND sparkles?) or you can choose them to reflect your intention, so you are literally bathing in your wishes. For instance if my intention was to cultivate vibrancy, I might choose orange and pine essential oils, maybe with a salt rub-down at the end of the bath, some stirring classical music and the early morning as the best time, followed by dancing, yoga or a morning workout. If, instead, I was nurturing my sensuality I might choose many candles, dusk, some harp or flute music and aromatic oil such as cinnamon.

If you're not a bath person or just can't find a bath: Adapt. Adapt it to a shower, a swim in the ocean or bathing your face, hands and feet in a bowl of warm, scented water in front of your Altar – you can still have candles, music, warm towels, an intention...

The Painted Body
Time: At least an hour
You will need:

- Either body or face paint, clay or henna (which will leave a stain for a number of days)
- Your Journal and pen

Use a henna paste, colored face paints, clay or earth mixed with water or oil to paint your body. Or give up on subtleties and just go for mud! Do it in your house or garden or outside in a safe place; either alone or with friends. Decorate just your arms and face, or take off your top (or all your clothes) and see what you can create! Write or draw in your Journal afterwards – or take photos.

The Edible Body (for the adventurous)
Time: At least an hour
You will need:
- Edible, bite-sized treats
- Liquid chocolate or other sauce (passion fruit glaze, perhaps?)
- Cream optional

Friends of mine have done this, though I never have myself (but it sounds good!)

Arrange your naked (or nearly naked) body comfortably on a sarong or old tablecloth and then decorate as you might a cake! Use bite-sized pieces of fruit, melted (but not too hot) chocolate and whipped cream.

Obviously it's best to have someone else decorate you – perhaps the same person who's invited to the feast, afterwards. You can do this with your lover, a group of women friends... or if you really want a sacred ritual, dedicated only to yourself and the Goddess, decorate the parts of yourself you can reach with a modest amount of edible decorations and then eat them, enjoying the sensuality of your lips, tongue – and maybe teeth – on your skin.

I am loving my body more as it is – I have stopped this habitual shaving of legs and armpits – I don't wear perfumes as I used to – I am accepting and enjoying my body's natural smells. And increasingly gone is the want to be thin – I am loving my womanly curves and the softness of me. I am loving to see softness and curves in other women – reveling in women who can be their natural self – and loving the differentness of each body.

Catriona

Preparation for Dancing the Body

For this Fifth Cord, try to remain with the body. That means if you start getting caught up in how your body or bits of your body look; grab hold of yourself and haul yourself back. Remember this: Skin, bones, muscles, blood. Skin-bones-muscles-blood – the human body. A woman's body. The whole of it. All together. The body-being. Be disciplined and see if you can slip through the net we have been so well taught, that the body is the reflection of its outermost layer in the eyes of someone else or our own critical, culturally-trained eyes.

Try looking at others this way – a child, your lover, a stranger in the street, someone you really dislike – as skin, bones, muscles, blood. As body. Record any thoughts or understandings you have throughout this section in your Journal.

Time: Allow an hour
For the Fifth Cord you will need:
- Comfortable, lightweight clothes to wear (of course you can also dance nude)
- Three 'sets' of music, each at least 10 minutes long. They all need to be good dancing music but choose different music for each section. The first set (which can be composed of more than one track) should be rhythmic, fairly fast and with a strong beat. The second set should be uplifting and can be demanding and varied in volume and energy. The

third set should be much more gentle, ecstatic, reflective or meditative; so long as it's not too slow to dance to.

- The Fifth Cord – choose a color that represents your body – maybe you will choose a color you love to wear, or a color you associate with the fifth chakra or the earth.
- Your Aphrodite Altar
- Your Journal and pen

You can share this dancing with a woman friend or friends. They don't have to do the whole process you are involved in, but make sure they know you are in a ritual and shouldn't be interrupted.

The work for the Fifth Cord is all in dancing, so have a good selection of music available. You may wish to read through the directions and then pre-record your music, so you don't have to change discs partway through, or you may wish to be more spontaneous, choosing your music as you go. For this process, unlike many of the others, I don't use music with any words or vocals at all – I want the experience of just my body with the music.

I just loved the dancing, I really felt ecstatic during the dances for the Fifth Cord, on the verge of orgasm.
    Diane

The Fifth Cord: Dancing the Body
This is the central work of this chapter.

Begin at your Altar. Cast a circle and raise energy as you usually do. Light candles, incense or lay an offering on your Aphrodite Altar.

Spend a few moments reaching out to the Goddess whose Girdle you are gathering, cord by cord. Name each one of your cords to yourself. Then do some gentle stretching as a warm-up; either following a system you are familiar with or stretching your leg, back, arm and neck muscles and shaking loose your limbs.

Place the other cords on your Altar and take up the Fifth Cord.

These three dances are the magical process for the Fifth Cord, so bring all of your intent and focus into them.

When you are ready start the first set of music. This music should be fairly fast and with a strong beat. Dance with it – push your body into the rhythm and work with the music – dance as hard as you can for the ten or more minutes your music goes for. This is the time for sweating your prayers. Perhaps you literally have prayers to sweat – *let me love and appreciate my body – let me feel the body of the Goddess – let me dance my way into physical and sensual joy* – or perhaps your dance is a wordless place of strong physical activity, where the body speaks its own language.

Dance each piece of your body separately, paying attention to every part. Dance with your feet, your ankles, your calves... dance with your buttocks, your back, your shoulder blades; your hair, your face, your head. You can dance with the Fifth Cord as a way of highlighting and praising each part of your body.

When the music stops, or the time you have allotted to the first section is up, pause only briefly as you change the music to the second set. This music is more varied in volume and style; let it take your body and transform your dancing. Dance now with your body as a whole thing; one beautiful, unique body, dancing for itself and as itself. Feel your muscles, flesh, bones; feel your breath and blood and heartbeat. Feel the music lift you, drop you, swirl you... dance through tiredness and beyond tiredness; find the place where the music carries you.

When the second set of music finishes, or the time you have allotted to the second section is up, pause again only briefly as you change the music and take a few deep breaths.

The third piece of music is gentler, but continue to move your whole body. By now you may have moved through stages of awkwardness, of exhaustion, of absorption but continue on. In this last piece, try to feel your body as the body of the Goddess. Invite her in. Maybe you will feel her in the lift of a thigh, in your arms as they sweep through a wide circle or in your feet. Maybe she will infuse your body or a long-familiar feeling will claim you and you will recognize her.

When the third set of music finishes you can sit or lie down if you wish. Hold the Fifth Cord and allow the gradual return of words and ideas to your mind. Choose a word, a name for your cord that describes your body. You might choose *lithe; whole; sacred; joy; power; dance.* If you cannot think of a single word that encompasses your experience, name the cord *body.*

Now that your cord is named, place it with the other cords, either on your Altar or somewhere about your body. Record this process in your Journal – perhaps with patterns and colors, if words seem inappropriate.

Remember to close down your circle and ground the energy when you finish.

Further Dances with the Body

These are optional activities. They can be done after you have completed your Fifth Cord or at any time during the remainder of your work with this book.

Establishing Relationship with Body

Time: One hour
You will need: Your Journal and pen

Consider the basics of food, sleep and exercise. Assign a page for each of these things in your Journal. Divide each page into three sections: *At Present, How I'd Like It* and *Realistic Goals.*

A Sample Food Page:

At Present: Basically good food but not always at the best times. Tendency to have the same meals every night. Probably not enough fruit.

How I'd Like It: Good, varied meals at the right times. A proper breakfast every day. One to two pieces of fruit every day.

Realistic Goals: Move fruit bowl near computer. Make a list of meals for the following week each Sunday and shop for ingredients. Invite a friend over for a meal once a week.

A Sample Sleep Page:

At Present: Tired every morning and sleep in on weekends. Wake in the night when worried about work and can't always get back to sleep.

How I'd Like It: Sleep deeply and comfortably for seven hours every night. Lie in on weekends for pleasure, not to assuage tiredness.

Realistic Goals: Buy a really good pillow. Go to bed at 10:30 at least four nights a week. Drink soothing tea before bedtime.

A Sample Exercise Page:

At Present: Walk to work twice a week. Sometimes visit the gym on weekends. Feel unfit and wish I was fitter.

How I'd Like It: Exercise four to five times a week. Do a mixture of gym, yoga and strenuous walking. Go out dancing or hiking for pleasure.

Realistic Goals: Sign up for a regular weekly yoga session. Take the gym's ten day trial and use it. Ask a friend to go cycling/hiking/dancing at least once a month.

Come back to these pages in a set time – say, one month and also three months – and record your progress!

Discovering Body

In your Journal write about some part of the body that fascinates you. You may be moved to investigate it further – how exactly does this work? – or draw it, either creatively or technically. Write about how it feels to be the caretaker of one body, and in particular to be carrying the part you have chosen. What is it like to have this skeleton (heart/brain/blood…)? Do you feel any responsibility towards it? What other emotions do you have?

Creating Body

My body is the body of the Goddess – make a drawing or collage in your Journal reflecting this. You can use photos of yourself, pasted into your Journal. Chant while you work, even in a whisper, the words: *My body is the body of the Goddess.*

Gifting Bodies

Choose a physical gift your body would love – a massage, spa bath or a dance or yoga class. Give it to yourself.

Now choose someone close to you – a child, partner or friend – and give a gift to their body – a massage, a manicure, a sacred bath or perhaps a gorgeous, sensual feast.

Resources

- *Body of the Goddess* (song), Michael Stillwater.
  https://innerharmony.com/show_product.php?pid=1143
- *Divining the Body: Reclaim the Holiness of Your Physical Self,* Jan Phillips. Skylight Paths Publishing, 2005
- Gabrielle Roth's Five Rhythms Dance Music
- *Gyn/Ecology: The Metaethics of Radical Feminism*, Mary Daly. Beacon Press, 1990
- *Maps to Ecstasy: The Healing Power of Movement*, Gabrielle Roth. New World Library, 1998
- *The Lesbian Body*, Monique Wittig. Beacon Press, 1986

SIXTH STRAND: RED WOMB

Once a month I realize power lies in the womb, blood and magic. It's when I realize why women are women and why we're basically mothers even though we might not have kids yet. It's an incredibly powerful thing to accept this red color as what makes us alive.
Artemesia

Women are born with wombs, whether they ever have pregnancies and give birth or not. Fertile or infertile, straight or lesbian, virgin, celibate or sexually active, women have a relationship to their wombs through the menstrual cycle. Some women appear to have an easy time of this, whilst others suffer cramps, pre-menstrual tension, irregularity, difficulty in conceiving or unwanted conceptions.

Monthly bleeding signifies the body's potential to contain and nurture new life. Many women consider the birth and raising of their children as one of their great achievements but other experiences have come to be viewed as part of women's fertility; artistic expression, a career and nurturing others are some of them. It is no coincidence that both the onset of menstruation and menopause – as women step into and out of the fertile part of their lives – are accompanied by huge emotional impact and social significance, as well as hormonal and physical changes.

One big change for me was an ability to really feel comfortable and accepting of menstruation – I had such a lot of shame in regard to this as a teenager and that still remained – or rather was left unquestioned – even after birthing three babies and being a nurse for twenty-five years. So bleeding is no longer in the dark – hidden even from me.
Catriona

My Red Fertility

I used to be proud of my womb's history.

I never had an unplanned pregnancy. I always said *only one pregnancy and none by accident,* celebrating my perfect record of contraception. But now, forty-four at the time of writing, I look around and it seems those of us with *perfect contraception records* don't have many, any or enough children (by our own count). Many other women, with less *perfect* contraception, ended up having children at difficult times, too close together, with unreliable partners or as single mothers when they weren't ready and didn't have the material resources, emotional and practical support for those children. And I don't know that their lives have been happier – certainly they seem to have been harder – but they have ended up with more children.

My generation appears marked by women who either missed out on having the children they longed for or who had them and then struggled to bring them up without a partner. At times I feel almost guilty over my one child, knowing so many women who desperately wanted even one. But that guilt doesn't assuage my longing for the ones I didn't have. Yes – I waited for a relationship where a baby would be welcome. Yes – I had opportunities when I could have got pregnant to the wrong person or at the wrong time – but I had done it the hard way once, bringing up a child largely on my own and was determined not to do the same thing twice. So I waited.

I've spent ten years wanting a second baby, in turns obsessively; quietly; determinedly; searingly and I've gone through many, many letting go sessions over it. Having longed for it all these years but not done it, I've eventually had to accept my actions and decisions led me to have only one child. In effect, I chose not to have that second baby. Not through lack of desire, but lack of circumstances.

When I was nineteen I learnt the Billings Method, developed by Drs. Evelyn and John Billings and taught – to anyone who wants to learn it – by Catholics, in a convincing attempt to re/discover natural conception and contraception. The Billings Method involves understanding the mucus secreted by the cervix into the vagina. Each woman has a mucus pattern of her own, that by extended study one can familiarize oneself with and – if you follow the instructions – use as a basic, no-fail contraceptive. The same information can be used for pin-pointing the most likely times for conception.

I used other contraceptives as well, but all those years I have been following Billings. I can't not do it. I learnt it so well, so young that even walking down the street, even in dreams I could tell where I was in my cycle. And I was blessed in that, until a few years ago, I had an amazingly regular, co-operative and easy-to-read cycle.

To begin with, I learnt Billings as a contraceptive. But by highlighting my fertile and infertile times I came to understand my own cycle much more clearly, including my cycle of desire. It was incontestable that from the night before bleeding, all the way through the first half of my cycle (until after ovulation), I felt an increasingly strong physicality, sensuality and sexual desire. Until I was about thirty the few days leading up to ovulation was marked by the secretion of fertile mucus (which is structured in a way that assists sperm swimming up and through it) in such quantities that at times it would be sliding down the insides of my thighs. Unlike mucus at other times of the cycle (which can be sticky, 'flat' or just liquid) this fertile mucus is clear (instead of opaque or white) and stretchy; slippery; almost ropey in consistency.

It usually felt sexy and I thought any lover would be incredibly turned on by it – just its wetness and slide, let alone knowing what it signaled in me. But I picked a series of lovers and partners who, for reasons of their own, weren't much into sex. Not only were they not into my fertile mucus, they didn't much like my fertile time at all – they preferred it when I wasn't so sexual and possibly they even preferred it when I didn't really want sex at all.

Sometimes I have been wary of that mucus and its fertility; as a young woman wanting to avoid pregnancy and also after my son was born, when I was amazed and appalled at how my body resumed full fertile cycles when my baby was six months old (how could you want to do that again, right now?) At other times I spent long years wanting to revel in it but either having no lover, or a lover who wasn't interested. And I went through a period of so much grief and longing for another baby that each fertile time was an excruciating reminder of what I didn't have.

I realize now I have *never* celebrated that beautiful, amazing fertility. I have been in avoidance or angst or longing over it, one way and another, my whole fertile life. And I don't have much time left. Sometimes I hardly notice how different my cycle is from when I was twenty-five or thirty-five; each cycle still has the same pattern and Billings is not to do with counting days. But recording my bleeding dates I realize my cycles have become irregular; shorter and shorter, then long and now all over the place.

I'm incredibly glad I didn't wait for a man to be ready to have my one baby. I would never have had a baby at all, had I done that. So why have I waited all these years for a lover to celebrate my fertility, my fertile sexuality with me? Yes, I wanted to share it; like I wanted to share a baby. After I had my baby, people shared it with me – not before. Perhaps no one wants to celebrate this fertile sexuality with me before I am celebrating it myself? And even that is beside the point; obviously I should just celebrate it because it's mine and I want it celebrated.

It feels as much like mourning as celebration, these days I have devoted over the last few months to celebrating it. I can't have one without the other, perhaps, at this stage of my life; I am too aware of the conceptions, pregnancies and babies I haven't had. So it seems a cruel irony to be celebrating fertility, but brave and necessary as well.

These last few years I am even more aware of the contrast between making love during my infertile and fertile times (about the five days or so up to and including ovulation). At these times my skin has an extra layer of sensitivity, so all touch is a seduction; each piece of skin comes alive and responds. It's not just that my body opens more readily; softens, responds, moistens, stretches; it's the level of absorption I have with this process.

During other times of the month my mind can flit out of love-making onto a recent conversation, a list of things to be done, some irritation or discomfort but during the fertile time I am swamped by the delicacy and immediacy of sensation. It claims me utterly and love-making is like an orchestra. I wouldn't even want it all the time; the more focused, delicate sensuality has – although less innate passion – more intimacy, more relatedness. But I imagine soon, through menopause, I won't have it at all, ever again. Not in that way; beyond my will, just from body/hormones/womb. Maybe there will be some rememberings of it, in moments, at times; but not days of it I can sink into, reveling in thick sensuality that wraps me in tides of sensation.

I try to imagine something – and I don't know what – will replace it; some deeper mystery I cannot even be aware of, this side of menopause. I heard one post-menopausal woman talking eloquently about not being driven by the body into sex or intimacy. She claimed instead to gain a deepening awareness of choice and so her empowerment, as well as a truer sense of connection in intimacy with her partner.

Meanwhile, I am doing my best to celebrate.

The work with binding the red cord enabled me to access and let flow my repressed early shame around the onset of my menstruation.
Deb

Hidden Within the Red Womb

Of the seven strands of Aphrodite's Girdle this Sixth Strand inevitably inspires the most grief. Grief over infertility, past abortions, lost children, dead children, hysterectomies, crippling menstrual pain, a yearning for babies that can't or don't happen for a variety of reasons. Our wombs are hotbeds of emotion and unexpressed pain. I wonder if being able to process these huge, life-changing issues more fully at the time of their experience would go some way towards healing our whole relationships with our bodies, sexuality and femininity.

Menstrual cycles are just that – cycles. Further, they are cycles of relatedness. They are linked to the moon and the tides of the ocean. Should we be living in a house with other fertile women, our cycles will relate to each other's. Unlike the linear vision we have of our lives – progressing from birth through to death along a straight line of important events – menstrual cycles remind us that life occurs round and round, in circles or spirals.

Apart from the day-night-day cycle, menstrual cycles are the most prominent reminder we have that things move in circles. They remind us we came from our mothers and they came from their mothers; they remind us of the full history of gestating, birthing and bleeding women. They remind us the ending of one cycle is the beginning of another and of our body's inescapable connection to life and death.

Although our culture celebrates cycles (birthdays, anniversaries, New Year and most religious festivals are all cyclic celebrations) we still continue with a linear model that brings great struggle and grief with it; insisting as it does on current successes, continual growth and the one-way street of life and death. We believe the death of a loved one will mean a future devoid of that person, because the moment in time when they died gets left behind as we travel ever onwards. Yet cultures that have viewed time as circular or cyclic have quite a different relationship to death. Even the way we bury people is an obvious contrast to ancient burials where people lie curled up, on their sides – as if placing them in the earth is returning them to the womb.

One woman I knew carried a debilitating grief over an abortion she'd had. It was not that she regretted it but she felt a shame and guilt over having cut short a potential life. When we began to speak of cycles and she realized that – however brief – the fetus had its own cycle of beginning, existence and ending she came into a more peaceful place. The circular model had given her what the linear model never could, a sense that this spark of life had its own belonging in the life cycles.

Women who've had hysterectomies when they weren't ready, didn't choose them or hadn't finished their child-bearing can also experience this pain of being cast adrift. Perhaps viewing the larger cycles of birth, fertility and death might assist them in finding their place within the generations of women of their family, tribe and even ancestral race. The experiences each woman *has* had, rather than the experiences they've missed out on can serve as a touch-point for receiving blessings from our wombs, instead of *the curse*.

Infertility, whether physiological or circumstantial can also lead to unending grief, regret and a sense of lost purpose, failure and unlived potential. This is rarely mourned or acknowledged the way the death of a child is, yet it can be as potent for those experiencing it.

We tend to ignore the fact that all children who are born will die. Each being has a cycle of life and death and these cycles are not arranged to our own choosing or our preferred imagining of the way the world should be. Even if our personal cycles and our family's cycles do not run to our preference, still we and they have been part of the larger cycle, as well as our individual cycles.

An artist friend of mine, whose only child died aged ten, painted a series of heart-rending pieces. They showed a woman shaped in a half-circle like a boat, or a crescent moon, with a child held within the scoop of her body. Thus the child's life is contained – both beginning and ending – within the life of the mother, who holds all of it in the shelter of her body.

I do not think this art or this understanding lessened the grief of my friend. I do think it helped her place her experience within the great cycles of life and allowed her to continue to hold it in a way that felt honoring to her. By acknowledging the cyclic nature of life we can hold it and be held within it, rather than moving on to progressively more distant places.

In the cycle of life we are always returning. Thus we may be able to hear the voices of our ancestors when we walk on their sacred ground and we can continue to feel the presence of loved ones, even after their death. Our fertility is a small piece of the earth's vast and rich fertility which births birds and animals, trees and rivers.

My womb has never been a safe, cozy place and is not promising to ever be one. It's no source of pleasure, although it reacts to pleasure in other parts of me. I have saved it from extraction once, but this does not make me feel proud or happy, because of all the pain that followed. Last spring new growths have been discovered and although I have matured beyond the unnecessary fears and angers of the process, I still feel scared of what might happen... I have begun to take it into my shadow work, so that at least I can look at it less as a victim and more like an explorer. How do I feel about the red cord now? I named it 'Completeness' and that is what my womb means to my femininity. I still have both and I still have to fight for their existence. I could as well have named it 'Struggle'.
Berin

Approaching the Red Womb
These activities are the lead-in to the Sixth Cord. Do both of them if you can.

It may be hard to visualize your womb, or even know exactly

where it is. Place your hands loosely, palms-down on your belly, with your thumbs meeting at your belly-button. Allow the first fingers of both hands to touch as well, pointing downwards. In the vulva-shaped space between your hands lies your womb, about two-thirds of the way towards where your fingers meet.

Womb History (Herstory)
Time: 30 minutes to an hour
You will need: Your Journal and pen

On a new page in your Journal write the history of your womb. Begin with its beginning, inside your mother's womb and continue through to the present. You may wish to make a timeline (or a time-cycle), with significant events listed by date, such as the onset of menstruation; any pregnancies; operations; childbirths; menopause – or maybe yours is a more poetic history, with descriptions of different feelings and events. Alternatively, you can draw a history; in cartoons, a mandala or any style that pleases you.

Looking at what you've recorded in your Journal, ask yourself what it shows you about your relationship to your womb. You may like to do a little nurturing of this relationship, or even mending, before going onto the Sixth Cord. Your womb might appreciate a massage, poem or healing meditation.

If it is very difficult, or impossible for you to write this history, use your Journal page instead to ask yourself about this missing connection with your womb. Why do you think this has happened? What feelings do you have about your womb? What feelings or attitude would you like to have towards this part of you? Try listing the gifts, and also the griefs, your womb has brought you.

Nest-Making

Time: One to two hours
You will need:
- Materials to build a nest
- Contents for the nest

You can use an abandoned birds' nest for this if you have or find one, or make your own nest. One method of nest making is to weave a small nest with grasses then pull some ribbons, feathers or leaves through the mesh. You can also make a felt or fabric nest, a paper-mache nest or a clay nest.

This nest is a representation of your womb. Think about where you might like to keep it – on your Altar, in a dark cupboard or outside in a tree – and how you would like to line it and what to keep in it. You can line it with some kind of down or fluff (cotton wool if you can't find anything else), bright scraps of material or soft grasses or ferns. Things you might place inside it include: Seeds or beads to represent your fertility; precious crystals to represent children you have had (or not had); symbols to represent creative projects you have nurtured or your future hopes. You can also place shells for Aphrodite; a tiny, sewn doll or heart; or small photos into it.

Sprinkle a blessing in the form of filtered water, or a few drops of your favorite oil or perfume or your menstrual blood onto it. Either sew it shut or leave it open – you can also weave or make a lid for it if you like.

Sit with your nest in meditation or ritual. Draw it in your Journal.

Now place it somewhere and visit it every day for a few days, or for a whole moon or menstrual cycle. Remember to give thanks for all the gifts your womb has granted you. If you like and it is appropriate, you may ask for a special wish to be granted. Never involve another person unasked in these magical wishes, requests or spells – it is highly unethical and considered to bring with it, at the very least, bad karma. Instead, ask the universe to grant you *a partner* or *a child to love, if and when appropriate* or *the return of my own sensual, body-delight.*

I had been desperate for a baby in my second marriage when I had to have a hysterectomy, so losing my womb was even more traumatic... At the start of the plaiting I found it very hard, sobbing, pain – hard to do the plaiting. As the time went on, the plaiting became easier, and rather than feel the pain for the lack of womb and baby, I felt joy for having had a womb and giving birth to my two children and having four grandchildren. A transformation from pain to joy.
    Annabell

Preparation for the Red Womb

The Sixth Cord, unlike all the others, is made by you; plaited from red wool to match the length of your other cords. Its color is red; red for blood, life, death; red for the womb.

This process, when it is working well, can take up to an hour. Many women take an hour and a half to complete it, so make sure you have allowed this time. It's not always women who are confident with their hands, or craft work, who do it quickly – a lot of emotion can come through as well as the technical challenges involved.

Some women go through tears and despair over tangles they create with this red wool, some begin so slowly they think they will never get to the end of it. But each woman eventually finds a way to create her red plait and plaits consistently and patiently enough to make a red, three-stranded plait as long as her other cords.

Keep a box of tissues, or some handkerchiefs near you – the whole point is not to stop, to keep going until your plait is complete, much as you do not stop during labor. If you must stop for a few moments, do not replace the activity with anything else; just sit quietly breathing with your eyes closed and then take it up again.

Time: Allow two hours, which includes dancing and Journal writing time

For the Sixth Cord you will need:

- Red wool – normal knitting wool or rug-making wool. Choose a strong red – I prefer bright red rather than dark.
- Measuring against one of your other cords, cut a length of red wool that is <u>two and a half times as long</u> as the cord. Then cut two more pieces of wool the same length as the first one. Put the other five cords away.
- Music to work to. I use Carolyn Hilliyer's *Blessed Be the Blood* from her album *Old Silverhead*. I put it on repeat, quite loudly, throughout the entire plaiting. By the end – having gone through stages of receptivity, irritation, sometimes ferocious anger and distress and finally a sense of peace and concordance with the process – the words pound through my blood; irretrievably drummed into me. Alternatively, you can chant or choose a song you think will convey the honoring of women's menstrual blood. Make sure this is not soothing music – it is supposed to be stirring, even provocative and demanding.
- Other music, for dancing to once you have finished the plaiting process. This could be Eastern, belly-dancing style music; world music with a strong beat or any other music you feel comfortable with.
- Tissues
- Your Aphrodite Altar
- Your Journal and pen

The most profound part for me was plaiting the Sixth Red Cord… I found it led me into a very inward space where I was able to thank my body for the brilliant work it has done for me in my life – especially my regular periods and my easy birthing of my two boys. I realized how little appreciation I have ever given to this part of myself – in fact quite the opposite – often finding it extremely messy and tedious and smelly.

I forgave myself for having such thoughts and blessed my blood.
  Gini

The Sixth Cord: Womb
This is the central work of this chapter.

Begin at your Altar. Refresh the flowers, light candles if you have them. You may wish to burn incense throughout this process; you can use it to remind you of being within a Temple. Cast your circle and raise energy in a way that feels best to you.

Spend some time with Aphrodite – either in thought, meditation or writing in your Journal; reflecting on your journey until now and preparing yourself for the Sixth Cord. If you have a statue or symbol of Aphrodite (such as special shell) on your Altar you may wish to hold it.

When you feel calm and centered turn your thoughts towards your womb. Place both hands over the womb area, below the stomach and take some deep, slow breaths.

Perhaps you no longer have a womb. Perhaps you are pregnant or longing for a baby. Maybe you are bleeding as you do this, or perhaps you have long finished bleeding. Perhaps your periods have always been difficult, painful or irregular, or perhaps you have hardly noticed them and they didn't interfere with your daily life. You may be a heavy bleeder, menstruating for five to seven days each month; or bleed lightly, only two or three days. You may have had abortions, miscarriages, live births or never conceived. You may view your womb as the centre of your creativity, your femininity, your fertility or simply as part of your body.

Think about what your womb has meant to you through your life and what it means now. Think about anything precious it has brought you and think also about any pains or griefs you have associated with your womb. Some of these thoughts will be matter-of-fact and resolved, whereas others may still be jagged with emotion – sometimes joy or hope, fear or pain. Pick out three of the strongest associations you have with your womb, to concentrate on throughout this process. They may be the names of your children, your wishes, your sufferings. For example, I might choose the name of my child and the words *longing* and *fertile*.

When you have these three words or phrases, take up your red wool. This is a bit like a task in a fairy tale; to transform these enormous lengths of wool into a plaited cord, the same length as your other five cords.

Knot the three ends together and find a way to secure them – under the leg of a table or a heavy book; between the toes of one foot or on a nail or hook, if you have a convenient one close by. If you are working to music, put it on repeat.

Plaiting the red wool is the magical step in the Sixth Cord, so bring all of your intent and focus to it.

Technical Advice for Plaiting Long Strands of Wool

- It's best to roll the three separate strands up into loose balls (or wrap them around pencils) to begin with. Then keep adjusting these balls of wool, rather than work with the enormous length of the wool, which tangles and knots very easily. Part of this process is learning how to do it in a way that works for you – sometimes there can seem to be as much unpicking as plaiting, and far more time spent untangling the ends than adding to the plaited length.

- Aim for a loose, even plait by pulling *away* and *down* from where the knotted ends are anchored and keeping as consistent a tension as possible. If your plait becomes very tight you will never get to the end of it. If you notice it becoming tight, check if you are pulling your hands out to the sides of the plait between each movement, and change this to pulling them downwards. The plait, whilst being loose, should not appear to have big holes in it; you want an end result that will operate as a single cord, not be looping all over the place.

- Once you get some length to the plait, move the point where it is being anchored – by wrapping the plaited length around your foot as you go, if you are holding the end between your toes; or by moving the plait further under the table leg, so you can still maintain a tension on the piece you are working on.

- It looks strange compared to the other cords but once they are plaited together in the final process, the difference is barely noticeable.

Magical Advice for Plaiting Long Strands of Wool

- As you plait, you can chant – either aloud or under your breath – the three words you chose to work with around your womb; or you can sing with the song, if you are listening to one. This will be an added focus; instead of allowing your mind to wander you keep it firmly with the process of plaiting, bleeding and your feelings towards your womb.

- If you continually plait too tight – or can't make it work at the top without tangling the bottom of the threads – ask yourself what it's about. Are you running into issues about control, responsibility, persistence, following instructions – and are these reflected in your life? Even without coming up with any answers, asking these questions can tease out difficulties, making the work easier.

- Many, many women can only make this process work after they have been through a major self-confrontation and taken in seemingly distressing knowledge about themselves. Yet these are the women who – afterwards – value their Sixth Cord as one of their favorites. I've seen other women – often very competent, self-assured women

– plait the whole thing straight through, with hardly any stumbles or correction but afterwards confess they hated it throughout and really had to win their peace with it.

Plaiting the red cord is a process that can really test your intent, focus and enactment. Remind yourself of these as you go along. If you are struggling, it may bring to mind other areas in your life which are a struggle, whether they are to do with your womb, your sexuality or some completely different area. Allow the plaiting, your consistency and dedication to magically shift your energy in that area, as the plait is created. Once the plait is as long as your other cords, knot the end and cut off the remaining wool.

Have a short break – drink some water, stretch – and then put on your dance music and dance with your red cord. Name your cord with the strongest word that came to you through the plaiting process. It might be one of the three words you started with, a word from the song you were listening to or a completely different word, such as *strength*, *flow* or *life*. If no other name comes to you, you can name your Sixth Cord *blood* or *womb*.

Place the red plait with your other cords – on your Altar, under your pillow, around your waist or in a special box or container. Take some time to record your experiences in your Journal.

Remember to close down your circle and ground the energy when you finish.

While plaiting the wool I was going through very different emotions, from aggression to tiredness, from elation to crying. I found this process very intense and came out of it with a sense of the essential mystery of my womb and my sexuality.
Miriam

Delving into the Womb: Further Work

These are optional activities. They can be done after you have completed your Sixth Cord or at any time during the remainder of your work with this book.

Staying in Touch

Commonly we are not very in touch with the processes and monthly rhythms of our wombs. If you are still bleeding, you might like to keep a moon calendar where you note your bleeding times, maybe along with dreams, sexual activity (or desire) and moods. You might be inspired to learn more about natural fertility control – either for practical purposes or just to become better in tune with your body.

You can place a cup, goblet or small bowl on your Altar as a symbol of your womb. Fill it with rainwater (or fresh spring water or herbed water) and add an offering of a small crystal, shell or a few flowers. If you are going through a pregnancy, menopause or any kind of distress associated with your womb you can work this more strongly, attending to it daily and meditating with it; as well as using it for a starting point in your Journal writing.

Womb Honoring

Think about how you would like to honor your womb and all it has brought you. This is especially important if you are past menopause. You might feel it to be an active force in your life, fuelling your creativity and sensuality, or other things. You may feel a part of you has died. You might choose to look at the children it brought you, moving around the world as their own beings.

Find some way to create an honoring of your fertility. Perhaps you will plant trees or herbs; make creative projects from embroidery to sculpture, cooking, writing or landscaping. Or honor your fertility through your relationships; whether with children, a partner, friends or strangers you reach out to.

Painting with Red

Time: 30 minutes to an hour

You will need: Menstrual blood or red body-paint or earth ochres

If you are a woman past her menses do this ritual whenever you feel is appropriate. If you have periods, do it during your period, even if you choose not to use menstrual blood.

You can do this outside (somewhere beautiful and private), in your bathroom or in front of your Altar. You might like to have a mirror nearby.

Take your clothes off. Begin by casting a circle, dancing or whatever you feel to do. Then paint your body, or parts of your body, in red designs. You can paint handprints, crescent moons, snakes or whatever you like!

Celebrate your red womb; all that it has given you and all that it means. Celebrate by dancing, feasting, sleeping, singing or meditating.

When you wash the red off, make the washing as sacred as the rest of your ritual.

Resources

- *The Billings Method: Controlling Fertility Without Drugs or Devices*, Dr. Evelyn Billings and Ann Westmore. Life Cycle Books, 2000
- Moon Diaries, Moon Calendars and Moon Charts are available which help you to record, honour and understand your cycles. Look for them in health food shops, alternative bookshops and on-line women's or Goddess sites.
- *Old Silverhead: Songs and Initiations of Womanhood* (CD), Carolyn Hilliyer. Seventh Wave Music, www.seventhwavemusic.co.uk

- *The Red Tent: A Novel,* Anita Diamant. Picador, 2007
- *The Women's Wheel of Life: Thirteen Archetypes of Woman at Her Fullest Power,* Elizabeth Davis and Carol Leonard. Penguin, 1997

SEVENTH STRAND: INNER MYSTERIES

I was worried about my own vagina.
It needed a context, a community,
A culture of other vaginas.
There is so much darkness and secrecy surrounding them,
Like the Bermuda Triangle,
Nobody ever reports back from there.
In the first place,
It's not so easy to even find your vagina.
Women go days, weeks, months, without looking at it.
I interviewed a high-powered businesswoman,
She told me she didn't have time.
Looking at your vagina, she said, is a full day's work.
Eve Einsler. *The Vagina Monologues.*

It can be difficult choosing words to describe women's intimate parts. Or, as Eve Einsler suggests, even finding them.

But can we walk proud as women if we can't name the parts that make us women? How can we talk about sex, or write about it in our Journals, if we can't describe those parts of our bodies that sex involves? How can a woman have a good relationship with her sexuality if she doesn't have a good relationship with her genitals?

If we want to teach a lover what pleases us, we have to understand those parts of ourselves. If we want to tell a young girl about her body, or a young boy about female bodies we need words to describe them. To be able to touch ourselves, even for pragmatic purposes (inserting tampons, never mind pleasuring ourselves) we have to have ways to relate to our genitals.

It was refreshing to be able to release all the negativity surrounding the
vagina. I have brought my daughter up to call hers a Fairy as these

beings are fun, mischievous, nearly always hidden, deliciously naughty, hugely magnetic, exciting, mysterious and inviting. I think that's a much better description!!!
    Shelley

Background to the Inner Mysteries

Women's genitals. These parts of our bodies hold the inner, sacred mysteries of birth and ecstasy. They are surrounded with cultural shame, objectification and uncertainty.

To begin with the words. In scientific terms women's genitals comprise: The labia majora and labia minora, the clitoris, urethra and vagina. Vulva is another word used to describe all the sexual parts of a woman. At least this is a step along from not naming them at all. Well-taught young boys and girls do – now – know the word *vagina* but how many know the word *clitoris*? In any case, many women object to these clinical terms as cold, awkward, or masculine-derived. Some choose instead to use the Eastern word *yoni*, or use a slang word such as *pussy* or *fanny* and abbreviate clitoris to *clit*.

The strongest term of abuse in the English language is not *prick* but *cunt*. This word had its origins in ordinary language as spoken by peasants and working people. D. H. Lawrence uses *cunt* in *Lady Chatterley's Lover* to harness an erotic force that delineates its speaker as earthy and primal and his lover as a woman rendered sexual by her response to his body and words. It is clear this language and the sexual acts between them remove her from the limitations of her upbringing, class and position. It's also clear that words commonly understood as derogatory can be – in another context – adoration.

Rita Mae Brown coins perhaps the most original description of a woman's vulva, *Rubyfruit Jungle*, in her book of that title. Original, vague and personal names abound in this absence of an acceptable common name for our genitals. What one woman thinks of as a term of denigration or abuse, another woman finds acceptable. We do not have a language in common for these parts of ourselves.

Women's understandings of the aesthetics of our genitals are even more conflicted than the words used to describe them. Within a few minutes I've heard one woman refer to them as beautiful, mysterious and delicate while another says she will never find them attractive or understand any attraction towards them. Like other parts of our bodies that have been pressured into looking younger than the woman they belong to (unlined faces, smooth legs, taut breasts, hair that never greys), to have a genital area shaved of pubic hair is now promoted as more feminine and sexier – that is, resembling a pre-pubescent girl rather than a mature woman.

The retail industry sells deodorants for intimate female parts. Some panty-liners and menstrual pads are perfumed. This is in spite of the fact that the pheromones in vaginal secretions are known to be a powerful attracting force. Musk (derived from animal sex glands) has long been held to be amongst the sexiest of perfumes. But we are taught to cover up our genuine scent as offensive and even sexually repulsive.

Statues and paintings of nude men show their sexual organs, whereas mostly a woman's are depicted as neatly closed; a delicate line down a raised mound. Exceptions to this, such as the Sheela-Na-Gigs (stone carvings whose hands hold open the lips of their vulvas, found particularly in Ireland and England) are considered shocking and – in the Sheelas' case – are often depicted as hags; the statement is about the raw power of life and death rather than feminine beauty or an ordinary woman's essence. We rarely see artistic visions of the entirety of the female body.

Georgia O'Keefe's flower paintings and Judy Chicago's art installation, *The Dinner Party* (delightfully described as *vaginal iconography*), are rare examples of art that depicts the exquisite detailing of women's sexual organs as beautiful, erotic and inviting. *The Vagina Monologues* by Eve Einsler – a piece of theatre often performed by ordinary women as well as by actors and celebrities – seemed determined to burst open the silence and neglect women's genitals suffer from in mainstream culture. The inclusion of the word *vagina* in the title and its continual repetition throughout the play eventually transforms the topic into one of ordinariness, as character after character talks about her vagina. As with Chicago and O'Keefe, Einsler gets beyond the shock factor of female genitals through sheer repetition. Then an appreciation of the work can begin; along with the belated acknowledgement that every woman on earth has one of these.

Of course vulvas and vaginas have long had a place in pornography and debate continues as to whether this oppresses or liberates women. Pornography operates within a society that does not worship women nor regard their natural bodies, including their genitals, as beautiful. Porn exists on the margins of social acceptability and it seems it's the forbidden nature of the imagery, rather than glorification of women's bodies that motivates it. So although porn does promote these images it is not fundamentally empowering to women, or in the service of women healing their relationship to their own genitals.

Ancient cultures did exist where women's wombs, breasts and genitals were honored as physical manifestations of the generative life-force. There have been times in human history when love-making was understood as engaging with the God and Goddess, on the deepest level possible. Different societies have made places for sexual healing; for the pursuit of tantric wisdom; for sex magic; for the worship of both divine and human sexuality. Cultures have existed where the Goddess' genitals were praised in the Temples and the streets.

In Chinese literature – modern as well as antique – women's genitals are described with such words as *open peony blossom, red pearl, the golden lotus* or *golden gully, the cinnabar gate* or *cinnabar cleft, the jeweled terrace* and other poetic phrases. These jeweled and flowered descriptions are laden with reverence, love and deep beauty.

Mesopotamia's Goddess, Inanna (known in Babylon as Ishtar), celebrated the fertility of the land, the people, the sheep – everything – as literally flowing from her vulva. The wealth of the land and the happiness and well-being of its people were understood to be the direct result of her love-making with her consort, Dumuzi. In Diane Wolkstein and Noah Kramer Samuel's translation of the poetry of this time, *Inanna Queen of Heaven and Earth: Her Stories and Hymns from Sumer,* Inanna refers to her vulva as "The Boat of Heaven… full of eagerness like the young moon"; her "wet ground" and promises her lover that grains and plants will flow from her womb.

Reading this poetry – and there's pages of it – the links between the sexual delight of the Goddess and her lover, the fertility of the land and the celebration of the people are straight forward. Inanna's vulva and womb are clearly where the wealth, abundance and joy of Sumer originate. The sexual love of the Goddess provides the whole land with nourishment and generative force.

Inanna's poetry is startling, four thousand years after it was written on clay tablets. It does not seem possible that the power and beauty of women's genitals was simply forgotten over the ensuing years. Further, those very places which worshipped this Goddess are now amongst the world's most prurient cultures – the lands of Turkey, Iran and Iraq.

When intervening events are considered – the tide of patri-archal religions; a culture stemming from Greek, Roman and Renaissance times; the advance of philosophical, psychological and medical sciences and the abstract separation of the mind and body – it looks as if one layer of propaganda after another has swept over humanity's consciousness of our origins. Human beings emerge from a woman's vagina. Perhaps our current unease with women's genitals is not due to our unfamiliarity with them but because of their intrinsic power.

This is the Goddess Gate
the gate of initiation
into Her holy mysteries
feel those tender juicy lips
directing your eyes, your tongue, your body
the most tender flesh awaits you
the moist lips of the divine kiss
are yearning for you
this is the gate of heaven
and the gate of earth
of the hidden treasures of life,
of the treasures of the trembling, sweating body
the gate to the hidden treasures of mystery
of soul connection
of divine wisdom through the folds of tender skin
this is the gate of darkness
of surrender to the unknown
to pleasures that cannot be anticipated
the pleasure of giving in to the burning and melting desire
this is the gate of the red flood
of the power of the moontide
of cosmic wisdom
of the cycle of all life
all life is in this swelling pearl
and in those sweet red lips
go and feel for yourself.
Miriam

The Power of a Woman's Genitals

In my twenties I worked on the edge of the sex industry. I sat at a telephone. Men rang up, paid for the service and then listened while I spoke an explicit sexual fantasy. Most of the men masturbated.

It seemed extraordinary to me – almost revelatory – that men found the mere description of a woman's sexual excitement – the imagination of it, the fantasy of it – so powerful they were willing to do this bizarre thing of paying money to masturbate over the phone. The business I worked for was very small and we prided ourselves on class and quality. My boss joked you needed a degree to be any good at the job; she held one in anthropology, mine was in education.

I've talked with women since who have worked as prostitutes or strippers from choice and they speak convincingly about power. This is very different from women who have no choice in the matter, whose experience in the sex industry is either largely or completely one of powerlessness. But – for some women – prostitution is a way of exploring women's power. Although superficially this power may be around money and the dare of dangerous living, a large chunk of it is to do with the power of women's genitals.

I felt working in the sex industry was at the cutting edge of patriarchy – nowhere else was the contract between men and women so clear: *I will speak for half an hour about sex and you will pay me an agreed amount of money.* And I found something tremendously satisfying and straight-forward about this contract. It seemed much simpler and more honest than almost any other female-male interaction. It crystallized and reflected in a microcosm the dominant paradigm perfectly – service-for-money – without any grey areas.

I did find it challenging to speak of my sexuality so forthrightly. On the phone I chose to tell my true age (thus, at twenty-five, I was 'older' than most of the women in the industry), my true measurements and my actual opinions, when anyone asked. I gave advice about what I liked sexually, how to talk to women and counseling on all sorts of topics, not necessarily sexual. On the phone I was forced to take the assertive role I had avoided in sex, romance and relationships.

The outcome of this job was I came to believe that men – at least ninety percent of those I talked to – loved women, loved women's bodies, loved women's sexuality and assertive women turned them on. This was revelatory to me; until then I had been sold on the critique of women's bodies and women's sexuality which women continually apply to themselves and each other. To be sexually admired – revered, almost – by so many men on such an impersonal basis changed the way I felt in the world. I never doubted my attractiveness as a woman again.

Embodying the archetype of the sacred prostitute is something many women feel called to do; perhaps particularly women who have experienced the magical, spiritual and transformative properties of sexuality. This archetype exists as an idea that in past times – perhaps the times of the Goddess Temples – sacred sex was revered as a healing modality. The women, or priestesses, who transmitted this healing were valuable members of society whose skills blended physical and spiritual ecstasies. In their dance and love-making they embodied the Goddess. Anyone lucky enough to witness or receive their healing was literally interacting with the Goddess herself.

In our world we all arrive somewhat damaged into relationships. In sexual intimacy we are presented opportunities and challenges to confront our own hurts, limitations and negative patterns and begin to heal them. In the absence of a Temple, where we could be trained in such arts or receive such healing, we often find ourselves in uncharted territory but with the support and love of our partner we can choose to undertake our own sexual healing. Although this can be fraught with difficulties and may require the support of books, counselors or wise friends, this healing has social approval as part of a sustained, long-term relationship.

Those who engage in sexual healing or the sacred prostitute archetype outside of a relationship meet a very different judgment. Think of the attitudes towards those beautiful, free and independent women who have sex *when they want to* with *whoever they choose*. Aren't they regarded as amoral, if not actually whores? Then there are women who seem almost too beautiful, so a man will do or say anything just to spend one night in her arms – regardless of her needs and desires. Others are women who cannot seem to hold a relationship; however lovely they are, one man after another leaves them. And there are also women who cultivate careful relationships with men unavailable for commitment, because it suits them to have sex with no ties.

There is a male counterpart to this as well; men who move through a series of brief relationships with women, connecting deeply and then being left by those women. Men whose relating adds to a woman's history of sexual trauma or grief do not fall into this category; men who are out to sleep with as many women as possible do not fall into this category; men who are opportunists and take whatever is offered do not fall into this category. Rather, these men will be like the women engaged in the sacred prostitute archetype; often completely bewildered as to why they cannot hold onto a relationship when they genuinely want one and seem to be offering everything.

There are women (and men) who are happy with this role of sacred prostitute. There are others who are happy with it for some part of their lives – perhaps whilst they are young, or mainly engaged with career, travel or personal journeys that do not allow room for a full partnership – but later on wish to develop more lasting connections, establish a committed relationship and possibly have children.

Sacred prostitution is one of the healing arts. Even in the absence of a Temple, it's a powerful path that's hard to break free from. Often it's easier to continue living the archetype that leads to intimacy, touch and love rather than abandon it for the unknown realms of a relating that does not involve – primarily, anyway – sexual healing.

I am one of those women, now in my forties, who found it very hard to create a relationship that would stick. No matter who I picked – straight or pagan men; men who'd never been married; men who'd left traditional relationships; men who claimed they wanted to settle down – none stayed. They had very little in common, these men. Just one thing, maybe; they were deeply wounded by the feminine. They could not seem to heal themselves.

Often, after they left me, they would quickly enter a relationship with another woman and move in together, have babies, commit to relationship. What was I doing wrong? Nothing. I think I was doing nothing wrong – but what I was doing wasn't going to lead me where I wanted. I wanted not to be a sacred prostitute any longer. Because those were the only relationships offered to me – and often, initially, I couldn't pick we were playing out that archetype again – it seemed they were the only intimacies, the only sex and the only type of relationship I could have. So I kept having them.

I did eventually get to a point where I was prepared to say, never again. It took me years to rewrite that pattern. To make such deep changes I've always found a total commitment is required. Within the container of the whole of my past, present and future I made the magical working: *I will never again go into relationship as a sacred prostitute, **even if that means I will never be in a relationship again.*** It felt as if I was abandoning all hope of intimacy, physical closeness and sexual connection, forever.

When I read about sacred prostitutes I feel a deep pang within me for the bravery, the skills and the yearning of those women. I know offering one's body freely is fraught with magic, danger and daring. I don't divorce what happened in the Temples thousands of years ago from what happens nowadays in any place where women and men offer love and sex as sacred healing and an expression of the divine. I'm not even sorry I stayed there for so many years, but I am pleased I've left.

Temple of the Goddess Aphrodite

O draw near!
Come unto the place of plenty!
Here is the entrance to the divine
The cave of the Great Mother
warm, embracing, pulsating.
Draw near & honor Her
Draw near & rejoice!
Here, my love, dwells plenty & prosperity,
Here in these sweet & liquid depths
May you be enfolded, surrounded, nurtured!

Here is the place of bliss
Here the golden lotus.
In these mystic oceans
bathe freely & rejoice!
Here is the glorious offering,
The sweet dews of heaven,
the mystic moonbeam pathway
to eternal delight
Come, my love, celebrate the Goddess,
the divine feminine!
Here in-spire the fragrant perfumes of sandalwood
and taste the sweet drops of divine nectar!
Deb

Approaching the Inner Mysteries

These activities are the lead-in to the Seventh Cord. Do both of them if
you can.

Inner Mysteries Meditation

Time: 30 minutes

You will need:

- Your Journal and pen
- Either read through the whole meditation first and then go through it remembering as much as you can; or pre-record it and play it back to yourself.

You can do this in front of your Altar or in your bedroom; wherever you are most comfortable. Casting a circle and raising energy are optional but you should offer a prayer to Aphrodite before you begin. Light a candle for her, smudge or otherwise prepare yourself, or dedicate a dance to the Goddess.

Lie down comfortably, but not so you will fall asleep. (Don't do this meditation at bedtime.) As you begin to slow and deepen your breathing take a couple of minutes to become aware of your body as a whole. Feel the weight of your body, feel your breath and then your heart-beat moving through you. Maybe you can feel your pulse throbbing or the blood moving through your fingers, neck, wrists or other points.

Place one hand, even briefly, on the crown of your head and recall your connection to Aphrodite, as you danced with the First Cord. Take a few breaths, remembering your feelings as you danced.

Then touch your hand to your forehead, in the position of the third eye. Imagine you are not only descending *down* the body, but descending *within* it as well, so each new point you touch is progressively deeper within yourself. Connect with the vision of yourself as beautiful, as Goddess, as you experienced it during the Second Cord or since then. Take a few breaths, re-enlivening that beauty.

Touch your hand to your throat and feel the depth from which your truth emerged when you spoke it during the Third Cord, and maybe since. Breathe deeply and imagine the clear channel that now exists for you to speak your truth.

Touch your hand to the heart area, either on the left side of the body or in-between your ribs. Take a slow breath whilst letting your shoulders relax and feel your heart as the very centre of your being. Imagine it glowing as it is infused with each breath and gently stretching and expanding.

Touch your hand to your solar plexus, about a hand's width above your belly button, and acknowledge your body. It is your body that carries all these other parts and it cannot be separated from them. Breathe deeply, feeling the living being of your body.

Touch your hand to your womb area, in-between your belly button and pubic bone. Imagine deep into the core of your body, the place where the womb is safely carried in the pelvic cradle. Once you were carried within your mother's womb, as she was carried by her mother and back through all time. Let your breath come and go as it will, feeling into this ancient line of mothers.

Touch your hand to your genitals; put your hand between your legs so you are cupping your whole upper body in your hand. Breathe in and feel the breath as if it spiraled down all the way through your body to this point. Allow yourself to approach the inner mysteries of your vulva. You might visualize this as entering a majestic hallway or watching the petals of a rose unfold; you might experience visions, sensations or emotions or receive specific information or messages.

The mysteries here are protected, cherished and revealed by all the other, outer layers of you. Not all emotions experienced in this deep place will be pleasant; grief, pain and confusion are as normal as wonder, gratitude and excitement. Whatever mysteries are revealed, allow yourself some time to acknowledge and honor them.

Then let your hands lie by your sides. Allow your breath to bring you back up through these layers of depth. Ascend up the spinal column step by step and be aware also of moving back towards the surface of your body and experience, as if you were putting your being together again.

Allow your breathing to return to normal and gradually become aware of the space around you. If you are near your Altar you might focus on that for a few moments to orient yourself. When you are ready, pick up your Journal and record your experiences. Remember to finish by grounding, acknowledging the Goddess, closing down the circle if you cast one and blowing out any candles.

Healing Deep Wounds

For many years I held enormous grief in my vagina. As soon as a man entered me sexually, I would burst into tears. It was as though making love triggered a body-memory so deep and entrenched that it had to be expressed, every time.

What swept through my body at those moments was grief, a tidal wall of grief. Something intrinsic was damaged, my trust in myself and my sexuality. It felt like that act, of sexual penetration, was the level at which I had been betrayed. I felt I couldn't recover. Even when I did seem to recover, this part inside myself – my vagina – kept reminding me of my terror, that another man might also leave me. That I could be forced again to carry that mixture of pain, desire, love and despair.

Jenny

It seems almost all of us have some kind of unhealed wound in the genital area. Some women carry physical wounds – results of violence, surgery, genital mutilation and disease. Women also carry emotional scars of rape, incest, abuse and – obscurely – emotional wounding that resides either in the vagina, in the reproductive organs or in the whole area of the genitals.

There are women who avoid all sexual intimacy, in order not to re-encounter the wounds they are carrying. There are women who protect themselves from becoming emotionally vulnerable in sexual interaction, so they don't have to visit those wounded places. There are also women who permit themselves to create, or remain in, sexually abusive relationships and possibly one level of remaining there is affirming – to themselves, at least – the truth of their wounds.

If you feel any type of sexual wounding is interfering with your ability to create meaningful, happy, mutually honoring and supportive sexual or intimate relationships, you should take action. Possibilities include counseling; support groups; self-help books; prayer and ritual; personal development and a variety of energetic, emotional and physical healing practices including Reiki; massage; flower essences and homeopathic remedies. If the wounding is deep and its repercussions have been persistent, it is most likely you will need a variety of these methods over a period of time.

You are the best guide for choosing appropriate therapies – but you in your powerful, truth-speaking self. If you would truly step through all seven gateways of this work, if you are dedicated to the Goddess, to loving yourself, to Aphrodite's Magic, then you cannot choose to tolerate or ignore this type of wounding; or to choose therapies that only quieten the symptoms, without addressing the depths.

The healing you undertake must be as strong as the wound you are carrying. At some stages it may seem almost as trauma-tizing as the initial wounding – the difference is the healing will allow you to move on, whereas sustaining the wound not only holds you still, but can continue to eat away at your self-confi-dence, your intimate relationships and your future.

You may choose to pause in your work here, to address issues of wounding before continuing on with the Seventh Cord, or you may choose to make the work of the Seventh Cord your first step on the path of sexual healing. The Seventh Cord and the completion of *Aphrodite's Magic* can be the beginning of a new phase in seeking to live your whole, celebratory and healed, Goddess-given sexuality.

I never felt degraded by the name calling but it made me realize that males were truly the weak ones for using such words as insults. After all they fear women and we're the scapegoats and yada yada... but if we don't explain to them how it works, how will they ever know? They're human beings after all...
Artemesia

Preparation for the Seventh Cord

Time: Allow an hour
For the Seventh Cord you will need:
- Several loose sheets of paper
- Flame-proof vessel and matches/lighter
- A variety of colored cords to choose from after the process; or else wait until you know the color of the Seventh Cord at the end of the process and buy it then.
- Dance music
- Love poetry, possibly of a sexually explicit nature
- Your Journal and pen
- Your Aphrodite Altar

The Seventh Cord: Inner Mysteries

This is the central work of this chapter.

Set up your Altar as you usually do. Cast a circle, light a candle, invoke Aphrodite and allow yourself a few moments of meditation, chanting or raising energy before you begin. Have your six cords on or near the Altar, as well as your Journal and pen.

Throughout the years you will have heard many different words and expressions used for women's genitals. These range from clinical, to slang, to swear words and abuse; words that obscure or prettify as well as words of honoring and love.

Take a loose page of paper – NOT a page of your Journal.

On this piece of paper write down all the words you have

found horrible, offensive, belittling, vulgar and abusive when they are used to describe women's genitals – your genitals. Write down all the terrible names, the ones that have hurt you and shamed you and cut you off from yourself. These might be words you have heard or read or even words you have used yourself.

Keep writing. Scrawl, inscribe, scribble but get those words down on the paper. Put them all down. It doesn't have to be neat or nice – this is exorcism. As you write each word, imagine the act of writing is removing it – permanently – from your mind, your memory and your body. If English is not your first language, write down words from both languages.

Once you have finished writing, read through the words once more. Those words are being cut out of you, with the act of writing them and they will never refer to any part of you again. You might want to say them aloud, spit them out or shout them away from your body and your self.

Now take your flame-proof vessel and scrunch your paper up into a ball. Place it in the vessel and light it (perhaps with your rage) and watch it burn. Do this safely. Move outside for this if you will set off a fire alarm inside, or if you need to for other practical reasons. Allow the fire to cleanse those words from your being.

You have now cleared an energetic space around the naming of your genitals. Soon you will be inviting in words, thoughts and images chosen by you to describe them.

Now move into the second part of the ritual. Begin by reading the poetry you have chosen aloud to your Altar. There are also some poems earlier in this chapter you may choose to use. Read slowly and with pleasure, allowing yourself to linger on the words and the feelings in the poems.

Following are three poems women have written for the Seventh Cord of Aphrodite's Girdle. Read them aloud, taking your time to hear and feel the words as well as speak them.

Have I loved you?
Have I loved me?
Have I named you?
I have named me!
My vulva
my clitoris
my vagina
what do I call you?
What have you been called?
"Heaven's Gate"
"Opening Peony"
My many petalled rose.

You have served me
well and faithfully
you have been quiet
and true
you have brought forth
my babies
have I said
thank you?
Did I know you
were my Temple?
Did I know you
through and through?
For all the times you've served me
Beloved
I call you.
Gini

cunt
inner sanctum
temple
secret sacred place

the inside of the inside
untouched place
> *oh I have welcomed in poets*
> *and adventurers and traveling princes*
> *but seek, ever seek the faithful one*
> *who would come to stay.*

My halls are satiny
> *blessed with the shining power of life*
> *my pleasure exquisite*
> *delicate with desire and love.*

Yearning, longing, frightened
I am beauty itself
I am diamond, I am pearl
at the centre
> *of the black universe.*

Jenny

Doux "bouton de rose"
Prêt à éclore
Attend la rosée
Attend la tendresse

Montagne de plaisir
Ondulant et se tordant
S'ouvrant dans le feu et la lave
Brûlant, attendant la pluie,
La caresse du nuage.

(translated)
Sweet rosebud
Ready to bloom
Waiting for dew
Waiting for tenderness

Mountain of pleasure
Undulating and moving
Opening in fire and lava
Burning, waiting for rain
And the sweet caress of the cloud.
Diane

Your task now is to write a poem about – or to – your genitals in your Journal. Make it as explicit as you like – no one will read it except yourself. In the poem find ways to name these parts of your body. Make up names or even new words, or use words you feel describe those parts of yourself. Names women have chosen include: *The Dark Gate of Mystery; Silver Flower; Beehive; Pearl of the Earth; Fireplace; Rose; Jewel; Hall of Pleasure; Lover's Delight; The Sacred Garden.*

Writing this poem is the magical step in the Seventh Cord, so bring all of your intent and focus to it.

Writing this poem is a sacred ritual. Write it in front of your Altar, or outside if you prefer. Decorate the page in your Journal where the poem is written. Then read it aloud – whisper it if you like – to your Altar and to Aphrodite. If you want you can choose later to read it to a friend, your lover or women's circle.

Finally, choose one of the names from your poem to be – for now – the name of your genitals, the most intimate part of your woman's body. Thinking purely about this name, the word or words you have chosen, pick a color that represents it (that you have not already got in your Girdle). This is the color for your Seventh Cord.

Name the Seventh Cord with the name you have chosen. Remember to close down your circle and ground the energy when you finish.

What a raw and wonderfully liberating experience it was to call out – cast out – the derogatory names I've heard and at times used myself for my most sacred and innermost doorway. The name I now choose to use is 'Golden Lotus'.

Tanna

Further into the Inner

These are optional activities. They can be done after you have completed your Seventh Cord or at any future time.

Vulva Portrait

Choose a medium – pastels; paint; collage; sculpture; quilting (or beadwork; macramé; knitting; glass mosaic or anything else you can think of) – and create a portrait of your vulva. You may need to study it for some time, using a mirror; maybe you'll take digital photos... The end result might be small enough to fit in your hand or you might make a Queen-bed sized cover. You can choose a literal depiction or one based on the feelings and impressions you receive through your genitals (after all, they are sensory-based rather than visual, for most of us). It might remain a private work in the pages of your Journal, it may end up on your Altar or you can place it in the entrance of your home.

Give Voice to Your Genitals

This is a writing exercise for your Journal.

Write the story of your life – from the perspective of your genitals. Write of discovering the pleasures of sensuality and love-making, of any physical or emotional traumas or pain and write also of your wishes and longings. You might write, also, of your own relationship to your genitals, which may have undergone many changes.

Once you have written the story, give it a voice by reading it aloud; to the mirror, your Altar or a special friend.

My Temple, my sacred Altar
A gift from The Goddess and to The Goddess.
Like a rose with such sweet fragrance
Gentle, erotic, unfolding beauty.
Your name claimed by so many for misuse
Yet glowing with love and unseen power.
Your strong curves and sensual mound
Now free from being hidden in shame
My doorway to the cosmos
My place of gathering energy and for reaching my ecstasy
A release of my passion, for touching the Goddess
My temple, my sacred Altar.

Annabell

Resources

- *Inanna Queen of Heaven and Earth: Her Stories and Hymns from Sumer,* Diane Wolkstein & Noah Kramer Samuel. Harper Perennial, 1983
- *The Dinner Party,* Judy Chicago. Installed Long-Term at the Elizabeth A. Sackler Center for Feminist Art, 4th Floor, Brooklyn Museum, Brooklyn, New York. www.brooklynmuseum.org/eascfa/dinner_party/home.php
- *One Hundred Flowers,* Georgia O'Keefe. Knopf, 1990
- *Sacred Sex: Discover the Secrets of Sexual Ecstasy,* Bernadette Vallely. Piatkus, 2003
- *Sex for One: The Joy of Selfloving,* Betty Dodson. Three Rivers Press, 1996
- *Sexual Ecstasy and the Divine,* Yasmine Galenorn. The Crossing Press, 2003
- *The Dinner Party,* Judy Chicago. Anchor, 1979
- *The Red Realm: Adventures in Sexual Spirituality,* David Deida. Plexus, 1999
- *The Vagina Monologues* (play), Eve Einsler. Villard, 2007

WEAVING APHRODITE'S MAGIC

I felt amazed as I started chanting the words I had worked with for each strand. The words formed almost a sentence in themselves; certainly they made sense even as they stood on their own.

Tanna

Congratulations! You now have all of your seven cords, each one a different color and representing an aspect of your unique sexuality.

You have a cord for your relationship to the Goddess; cords for your individual beauty; your truth; your heart; your body; your womb and your genitals. Each of these cords has a long history, going back to the time of your awakening sexuality, back to childhood, birth and even before birth.

They are not just lengths of cord, but items of beauty, power and magic. Each cord has your healing, your compassion and understanding anchored into it. Handling them, you bring more and more recognition, focus and depth to the issues that have arisen as you've done the work for each cord. Each has its own name, in most cases a single word. The names of your cords are as unique as the magic you are about to weave.

The naming of the cords and then their integration was a powerful and deeply emotional experience. I have realized that the Girdle and the objects I have adorned it with embody not only my sexuality but my whole outlook on life.

Helen

For this act of magic you will be concentrating on three different things: The technical aspect of plaiting your Girdle, a chant which is created by the names of your cords and the magic itself. For the magic you will need the three ingredients described in the Practical Guidelines at the start of this book: *Intent, Focus* and *Enactment.*

Broadly speaking, your magic is for the healing and celebration of your sexuality but you should also bring a personal intent to this work. Your intent may be the same one you began with, back in the early stages of the First Cord or it may have changed or developed since then. Your intent may be purely personal or you may add in a wish for other women, for the earth or the Goddess herself. You should set this intent very clearly before you begin work; writing it down, meditating on it or at the very least speaking it aloud to your Altar and the Goddess.

Staying focused is essential and you can assist yourself in this by making practical and supportive arrangements. Ensure you have enough time to complete the Girdle-making. Don't do it at a time you feel rushed, stressed, exhausted or unfocused. It's better to delay it than culminate all your work with a distracted piece of magic. Your focus will be held during this spell-weaving by the names of the cords; each time you pick up one of your cords you say its name aloud. Although this makes the beginning of the process slow, the order of the names quickly becomes a chant and the co-ordination of speaking the names, together with the motion of plaiting will hold your focus.

The third part of magic is enactment – actually doing it. This is where you bring together all those emotional and mental abstractions with the physical task of plaiting the cords together. If or when the plaiting becomes difficult, keep going. Technically, it is not as difficult as plaiting the Sixth Cord. Anyone who has managed to do that will find this process comparatively smooth. Many women find this weaving deeply moving, joyous and even ecstatic.

Think ahead and place whatever you might need to hand: Tissues, drinking water, a cushion to sit on. Pushing through this task, even if it seems to be killing you, is an essential part of giving your energy to the magic. Remember you are not just plaiting seven strands of cord together; you are weaving your sexuality into its new form. And remember all those fairy tales and don't give up until the task is completed!

My cords seemed to set themselves in a pattern that worked their own magick, overcoming the problems followed by positivity.
   Annabell

Preparation for Weaving Aphrodite's Magic
Note: the terms 'weaving' and 'plaiting' are used interchangeably to describe the following process.
Time: Allow an hour for weaving the Girdle, more time if you want to decorate it in the same session. The decorating can also be done at a later time.
For the Weaving you will need:
   - Your seven cords
   - Your Journal and pen (optional)
   - Dance music for when you've finished – joyous, expansive, wild
   - Read through the entire set of instructions before you begin. You will need to combine the Technical Information with the Magical Information when you are actually plaiting.

For Decorating your Girdle you will need a selection of:
   - Bells, beads, charms, feathers, shells with holes in them
   - Old jewelry, especially necklaces or pendants
   - Needle, cotton, scissors, strong thread to bind with

Weaving Aphrodite's Magic
This is the central work of this chapter.

Set up your Altar as you usually do. Cast a circle, light a candle, invoke Aphrodite and allow yourself a few moments of meditation or chanting before you begin. Have your seven cords ready. Unlike many of the other processes it is important not to have music playing, even in the background. You need silence to drop your magical spell into.

Very peaceful and lovely process. Like weaving my own life.
Artemesia

Technical Information for Weaving your Girdle
The Knot
- I place the first knot (which knots all the cords together) about 25cm (10 inches) down the cords, leaving the ends to dangle. If you leave this much at either end, you will still have a plaited Girdle that wraps around your hips, knots loosely and the ends will fall down your thighs. If you place the knot at the extreme end of the cords, your Girdle will be shorter (only slightly) but all plaited; or if you place the knot further away from the ends, you can make the whole thing even longer. It's really about how you want it to look and feel – all plaited, plaited with dangling ends or just plaited where it lies around your body with very, very long dangling ends.
- To assist with plaiting, you can place the knot under a chair or table leg, hold it between your toes or hook it onto a window catch or similar. This means you can pull against the plait, as you are making it, to get a consistent tension.

strength-goddess gate-woodlands-compassion-wholeness-juiciness-mystery - Miriam

The Plait
- Plaiting with seven strands is essentially the same as plaiting with three strands.
- Once the cords are knotted together at the top (or partway down their length), spread them out like a fan.

- Separate the cords, three to the left, four to the right, with a gap between.
- Pick up the cord on the furthest right-hand side and move it into the centre gap, then slightly to the left, leaving three cords remaining on the right-hand side.
- The cord you have moved is now on the inside of the left-hand side, which now has four cords.
- Pick up the cord on the furthest left-hand side and move it into the centre gap, then slightly to the right, leaving three cords remaining on the left-hand side.
- The cord you moved is now on the inside of the right-hand side, which now has four cords.
- Continue doing this, alternating right and left, always taking the cord on the outside, moving it to the centre gap and then slightly across, to join the three cords on the other side.

beloved-pearl-shining-power-depth-beauty-hope - Jenny

Extra Tips
- You can always tell which cord to move next if you keep the centre gap, it is the outermost cord on the side with four, rather than three, cords.
- After a very little while, you will also be able to tell which cord to move next by the color sequence created in the part you have already plaited.
- Lay the cords down neatly and securely – if you pull too tight the plait will buckle; if you let it lie loosely it won't hold together. Pulling *downwards*, away from the knot is more effective than pulling the cords out too far to either side.
- Unless you continually untangle the ends as you go, you will create a reverse-plait behind you which eventually will knot the cords, so you have to stop and unknot them

before you can keep plaiting. The best way to keep them untangled is to pull them all through completely, whenever you move them. Some women do this with every cord they move; I pull them all through with every second cord and some women only do it every third or fourth cord. You will find a rhythm that works for you and it gets easier as you get further along the plait and the cords become shorter.

- When you are nearly at the end, stop and measure the Girdle around your hips.
- Decide where you want the second knot to be – you can trim long cords to make both ends the same, or leave them as they are.

pleasure-reconciliation-celebration-fun-joy-peace-hope - Helen

Weaving the cords together with the chant is the magical step to create the Girdle, so bring all of your intent and focus to it.

harmony-grace-truth-passion-beauty-sanctuary-wonder - Shelley

Magical Information for Weaving your Girdle
Intent

- If you are unclear on your intent for the Girdle, do not begin yet. Sit quietly, meditate, chant or write in your Journal until you absolutely know your intent. It can be very simple: *To heal and celebrate my sexuality; To dedicate myself to the dance of Aphrodite* or more complex or specific: *To cleanse my body of the past and release my spirit into the fullness of my femininity; To dedicate myself to the joyous expression of the Goddess in my personal life and also in the world.* Do not hold onto an old intention if it is no longer what you wish to weave into your life. If your intention has changed, or is complex, you may choose to either write it down in your Journal or place it on your Altar.

- When you are ready (comfortable, with intention clear in mind) untangle your seven cords. Hold them in your hands and name each one to yourself. You may have to check one or more of the names at the beginning. Sometimes the name of one cord will change during this process, either consciously or unconsciously. If this happens to you, accept the new name unless you have a good reason for not doing so.
- Breathe in deeply, speak your intent aloud and knot all the cords at one end, putting your intention into the knot.

release-peace-sorrow-courage-joy-magick-sacred - Annabell

Focus
- Lay the cords out, as they emerge from the knot. They will rarely be in the order you collected them and even if you try to arrange this, they have a way of re-arranging themselves.
- Remind yourself again of the names of each of the cords; these names are a vital part of the magical process.
- Begin the plait slowly, naming each cord ALOUD as you pick it up and move it.
- If one of your cords has a lengthy name, for instance *sacred jewel of the shimmering clouds,* you may choose to shorten this to *jewel* for the purposes of weaving.
- Stay focused on the physical aspects of the task (moving the correct cords, keeping a consistent plait, not tangling the ends) whilst slowly getting used to the names of your cords, the order they arrive and the rhythm of your plaiting.

helder zicht-kracht-waarheid-openheid-sensualiteit-volledigheid-vuur
(clear vision-strength-truth-frankness-sensuality-completeness-fire)
- Berin

Enactment

- You are creating a seven word chant that has your magic, your healing and celebration bound into it. This chant will form its own rhythm, cadences and possibly a tune, so you end up singing it.

- It is vital to name the cords ALOUD, even if whispered. This action is sending your magic into the world and binding it into the Girdle. If you say the words only inside your head, the magic will not go forth in the same way.

- Most women forget one of the names of their cords, even continually. Ask yourself what significance it may have, to forget the name of that particular cord. After a while you will remember it.

- If you have written the names of the cords down, to look at as you go, get rid of this paper as soon as possible. The magic is about dragging those names out of your innermost self, which is a completely different process than reading them from a piece of paper. Be patient with yourself, be strong with yourself and pour yourself into this weaving magic.

- You may have to stop several times to untangle your cords or to unplait, to correct a mistake. Persevere. You have very nearly completed Aphrodite's Magic. You will pick up the chant again and it gets easier as the cords get shorter.

- If you waver, remember your intent. Stop and speak it aloud again if you have to, even several times – shout it out if it helps!

- When you get to the final knot, speak your intent again with the fullness of the power you have gathered through the plaiting.

beauty-force-love-courage-joy-power-rosebud - Diane

Dancing

When your Girdle is finished, it's time to dance. Take off as many clothes as you feel comfortable with. You are dancing to Aphrodite, so then take off one more piece of clothing!

Knot your Girdle around your hips, put your music on and dance to Aphrodite and yourself.

If you choose to decorate your Girdle right away, you can save the dance until after you have done this. If you're planning to decorate it later, make sure you dance at least one dance with your completed Girdle before you finish this session.

I keep mine above a doorway near my bedroom – a reminder and an amulet – I have worn it when alone – I will dance naked or clothed with it around my hips – it brings back the feelings of my womanliness – the essential feminine in me…

Catriona

Journal

Record your seven word chant as it came out during the weaving and anything else you would like to remember about the process. Draw yourself wearing the Girdle, or just the Girdle itself! This also can be done after the decorating, if you plan to decorate as soon as you've finished the plaiting.

If you are not going to decorate your Girdle immediately, make sure you close down your circle and ground the energy.

love-gentleness-truth-joy-thanks-scarlet grace-beloved - Gini

Decorating the Girdle

You may choose to decorate your Girdle as soon as you've finished plaiting (and stretched and drunk some water!) or maybe you will do your dance and Journal and come back to the decoration another day.

The decoration will be as unique as you – some like it elaborate; some simple. Some women make their Girdle noisy and colorful, others symmetrical and delicate; some like it heavy, to swing as they dance and others keep it a simple belt that can be easily worn.

Some ideas are:

- Cut the ends of the cords to different lengths and bind or tie shells, bells, feathers or pendants onto individual ends.
- Unravel the ends of the cords to make a multi-colored fringe.
- Weave a necklace or strand of beads through the plaited Girdle.
- Attach a necklace or pendant to the Girdle so it hangs down in a v-shape over one hip or in front or behind.
- Sew tiny charms, beads or sequins onto the Girdle.
- Attach a belly-dancing chain or similar in half-loops along the length of the Girdle.

The Girdle I made evolved as a colorful miracle... It is so beautiful! The making of it seemed mysterious in itself... the colors blending and the overall effect changing as they chose themselves. The threads are strong, vibrant colors, some darker, some paler, each with great character, different textures. I keep mine on my shrine at home, or sometimes by my bed, or thrown over my bedroom chair, even wound around my big wooden Buddha. I wear it now and then and thought of it just this morning as I lay in bed, waking up, intending to thread it through the top of some white summer trousers instead of a belt. It helps me to remember my radiance, which sounds boastful, perhaps, but it is true. I so easily forget... and if I allow myself to shine it lights, lightens, the experience of everyone around me. I know that and so does my Girdle!
Kate

AFTERWORD

LIVING WITH APHRODITE'S MAGIC

I still have this very beautiful Girdle, and it has come with me every-where I lived ever since. It normally lives in my bedroom... It has been very special to me... almost as a portal to the Venus dimension!
  Golden

If you have worked through this whole book and now have a beautiful, unique Girdle woven of Aphrodite's Magic to adorn your Altar, body, bed... what now?

For all my life I felt guilty, dirty, sinful about my sexuality, about having desires, lust and pleasuring myself... hence I never experienced the depth of complete pleasure because of this! Since my journey with Aphrodite's Magic I've realized that I'm a grown and very attractive woman who deserves to be pleasured and loved and honored and my most significant realization was that I've allowed others' prejudices to come between my self and one of the most wonderful physical, emotional and spiritual journeys we can undertake – as a woman in a loving, respectful, sexual relationship... I have been reborn.
  Tanna

Review Your Journal
Make some time to read back through your Journal, from the first page through to the last. Choose some things from your writing to take forward with you, into the future. These may be insights you had, poems you wrote, exercises you want to complete or rituals you'd like to do again. Bookmark the pages or make a note of these things you are taking on past the original process.

  Create an end-page of the Journal (even if you haven't

filled all the pages). On this page acknowledge the journey you've undertaken and offer your thanks to the universe, to Aphrodite and yourself. Let the end-page be a spell of completion.

I still have the Girdle. It's in my room as decoration. I haven't worn it a lot, but having it around reminded me of its power and filled me with it. It helped me a lot, even though I didn't need to wear it for that. It's one of those subconscious things...
Artemesia

Close Down Your Altar
At the beginning of this process you set up a special Altar to Aphrodite. Now is the time to decide what to do with it.

You may choose to leave it in place, especially if it is outside where it can easily become a permanent Altar to the Goddess. You may choose to take some items from it and place them on your main Altar, while packing away the rest of it. You might choose to continue with your Aphrodite Altar, changing it in response to whatever's happening in your life.

Whatever you decide, take a few moments first to sit with your Altar, recognizing the anchor it has been for your work. Light a candle and then blow it out, or do something else to symbolize the completion of your original purpose for this Altar. Any offerings you made to the Goddess should be disposed of in an appropriate way: Burn, bury or give them away.

Continuing Issues
Ask yourself if you are left with on-going issues, after this work. These could be such things as having awakened an old hurt that now seems active again; creating questions about your life that are disturbing or you don't know how to resolve; drawing your attention to an unhealthy pattern or relationship or powerful emotions you can't seem to integrate.

If this is happening for you, I encourage you to take action. Waiting for such things to 'settle down' is not resolving them but merely hiding them under a veneer of ordinary life. If you doubt this, re-read your intention and remember what you asked for. These issues are probably standing in the way of you fully achieving it, which is why they have arisen and why they won't just go away.

There are many wonderful books that deal with an enormously wide variety of issues and can offer support when you are going through something on your own. Used in conjunction with personal work, other support and a clear intention to heal, such books are a great resource. Some of them are listed at the end of the chapters for the different cords. Many others are only as far away as your local bookshop, library or internet browser.

Your Journal, your Altar and your spiritual practice may all assist you, whatever is arising in your life. However we often need to go further, to seek out appropriate assistance and ask for help. There may be friends you trust, or maybe it's appropriate for you to visit a professional counselor or find a support group that deals with your particular issue. Trust the process that has taken you this far and take the next steps that are needed to ensure your full healing. Grief, letting go and dealing with painful issues are all a part of celebrating life and the area of your sexuality is no exception to this.

If strong issues have arisen concerning your sexuality, this will obviously affect any sexual relationship you are in. Talk with your partner or lover about what is going on for you. You may choose to seek relationship counseling or to undertake some healing or learning work together, such as attending a workshop on communication skills, tantra, or any other field you feel is appropriate.

For me it was the start of a journey to open up to the Goddess within and my sexuality, hence I have removed all distractions from my life to deal with this.

Shelley

Wear Your Girdle

You might wear your Girdle to a party, ball or special event. You can wear it to rituals or in circles. You can wear it for your lover, or for yourself; naked or with clothes. Dance with your Girdle, either alone or with others. Wear it at night if you want to dream of love, or place it under your pillow. Wear it to the beach under a full moon. Wear it to remind you of the Goddess, the divine feminine that is also part of yourself.

You can keep your Girdle in a box, on your Altar or strung up in your bedroom. It might be so private you never show it to anyone, or you might want to display it proudly. If you've made the Girdle in conjunction with other women, throw a party when you've all finished and wear your Girdles; dance and feast together.

When something significant happens in your life – the birth of a child, an important anniversary, the death of a loved one – you can add a charm or special bead to your Girdle. Let Aphrodite's Magic continue to weave through your life. You have created a powerful magical item; use it for its purpose of healing, celebration and connection with the divine feminine.

Dance on!

When I wear my Girdle I know that I'm ready to engage with my femininity, not to hide behind my rationality, not to do what is useful, but what is beautiful. When I wear my Girdle, I've taken the time and space to be with my self, to acknowledge that underneath everything there is eternal beauty; the sensuality that can be hidden but never destroyed, not by betrayal, abuse, disappointment. I usually keep my Girdle in the drawer under my Altar, wrapped in a red shawl, but when

I wear it, I feel that Aphrodite is within me and always has been. I wear it for my solitary Beltaine ceremony, for belly dancing and often for loving myself, for giving myself pleasure under the moon. My Girdle is very colorful, as I am, and on its ends are various Goddess pendants that swing when I move. They are quite heavy so that I really feel the Girdle when I wear it.

Miriam

About the Author

Jane Meredith is a Priestess of the Goddess. She lives in Australia and works internationally. Her workshops include *Aphrodite's Magic: Healing and Celebrating Women's Sexuality.* Jane is passionate about ritual and mythology, magical living and the evocation of the divine.

Jane Meredith's website is: www.janemeredith.com
She can be contacted at: jane@janemeredith.com

BOOKS

O is a symbol of the world, of oneness and unity. In different cultures it also means the "eye," symbolizing knowledge and insight. We aim to publish books that are accessible, constructive and that challenge accepted opinion, both that of academia and the "moral majority."

Our books are available in all good English language bookstores worldwide. If you don't see the book on the shelves ask the bookstore to order it for you, quoting the ISBN number and title. Alternatively you can order online (all major online retail sites carry our titles) or contact the distributor in the relevant country, listed on the copyright page.

See our website **www.o-books.net** for a full list of over 500 titles, growing by 100 a year.

And tune in to myspiritradio.com for our book review radio show, hosted by June-Elleni Laine, where you can listen to the authors discussing their books.